Restoring
the Foundation
of Civilization

Restoring the Foundation of Civilization

GOD'S GOVERNMENT OR CHAOS

Gary DeMar

THE AMERICAN VISION
Powder Springs, Georgia

Published by The American Vision, Inc.
PO Box 220
Powder Springs, GA 30127

www.AmericanVision.org

Cover design: Joey Nance
Typesetting: Kyle Shepherd

Printed in the United States of America

Scripture quotations are from the New American Standard Bible.

Paperback ISBN: 978-0-9840641-0-6

Published in the United States of America

Contents

Introduction

Samuel Clemens, better known as Mark Twain, wrote the following concerning reports that he was seriously ill and near death (it was his cousin): "The report of my death was an exaggeration." A similar thing can be said about Western Civilization. It may be ill, but it's not dead. The enemies of Western Civilization are on life support because they are using force to implement their ideology. This is a sign of illegitimacy, desperation, and failure to change people's minds by reasoned discussion. The Apostle Paul writes the following about the end-point of unbelieving thought: They are "always learning and never able to come to the knowledge of the truth. But they will not make further progress; for their folly will be obvious to all...." (2 Tim. 3:7, 9).

Consider what was taking place in Louisville, Kentucky. An activist group was "threatening Louisville business owners with possible repercussions if they fail to submit to their list of social justice-related demands. Phelix Crittenden, who is allegedly the 'lead supply organizer for BLM Louisville chapter,' created a group called 'Blacks Organizing Strategic Success [BOSS].'"[1]

---

1. "Cuban immigrant says activist group using 'mafia tactics' to intimidate Louisville business owners" (August 3, 2020): https://bit.ly/3cdGVF8

The group's demands included having a minimum of 23% Black staff and purchasing "a minimum of 23% inventory from Black retailers or make a recurring monthly donation of 1.5% of net sales to a local Black nonprofit or organization."

Failure to comply would mean financial repercussions from BOSS that could shut down the non-complying businesses through boycott efforts and negative publicity "by launching negative reviews and social media posts about the businesses." These types of actions are a microcosm of a larger problem brought on by attempting to effect cultural change via a secular power religion.

CHRISTIANS MUST ENGAGE THE CULTURE

The main reason anti-Christian-civilizationists survive and seem to thrive is that Christians have not built a competing alternative culture founded on the foundational principles found in God's Word and observable in His creation. Moreover, many Christians don't believe there can be or should be a Christian civilization, so they send their children off to the local government school that is anti-Christian, believing that facts are neutral and public education is free. Such thinking comes at a terrible cost. Actions taken by Christians can fix this problem by simple obedience to God's law. If wolves in sheep's clothing are a problem for the people of God, then what should we think of wolves who identify as wolves and want to supplant Christian civilization founded on the basis of materialist operating assumptions?

It hasn't always been this way. Winston Churchill, for example, saw the Battle of Britain as a struggle between the kingdom of light and the kingdom of darkness. "Upon this battle," Churchill said on the 18th of June 1940, "depends the survival of Christian civilization."[2] Elements of a Christian civilization were observable and fault lines were noted and remedied.

Christians have always challenged the world when it was deep in the stench of paganism and ideological darkness. In the past, such conditions have brought out the best in the Christian worldview and those who extended it to the broader culture. Christianity infused the world with the light of the gospel and its call for the redemption of sinners and their sin-stained world. This vision of Christianity seems lost on many of today's Christians.

Anti-Christians are killing off their future via abortion and choosing not to have children. Homosexuality and transgenderism (and all the other genderisms) are folly and self-destructive. When men and women are cutting off their genitals to identify as the opposite sex, we must ask whose civilization is coming to an end.

There are many Christians who will not participate in civilization-building efforts that include areas like economics, journalism, politics, education, and science because they believe (or have been taught to believe) they are outside the realm of what constitutes a Christian worldview: "Politics is dirty," "Jesus didn't get mixed up in politics," "Politics is about law, and Christianity is about grace," "Jesus is our Savior not government'" "Jesus said that His kingdom is not of this world," "The Christian's only task is to preach the gospel," "We're living in the last days," and so many more myths.[3]

2. Quoted in John Baillie, *What is Christian Civilization?* (London: Oxford University Press, 1945), 5.

3. See my book *Myths, Lies, and Half-Truths* (Powder Springs, GA: American

POLITICS IS ONE GOVERNMENT
UNDER GOD'S GOVERNMENT

The thing of it is, a biblical worldview includes politics, the civil dimension of biblical government and everything else. The British poet and literary critic T. S. Eliot (1888–1965) makes the point better than I can:

> Yet there is an aspect in which we can see a religion as the *whole way of life* of a people, from birth to the grave, from morning to night and even in sleep, and that way of life is also its culture....It is in Christianity that our arts have developed; it is in Christianity that the laws of Europe have—until recently—been rooted. It is against a background of Christianity that all our thought has significance. An individual European may not believe that the Christian Faith is true, and yet what he says, and makes, and does, will all spring out of his heritage of Christian culture and depend upon that culture for its meaning....If Christianity goes, the whole of our culture goes.[4]

The entire Bible speaks about the subjects of governments and politics just like it speaks about everything else. Abraham Kuyper (1837–1920), one-time Prime Minister of the Netherlands and Professor of Theology at the Free University of Amsterdam and editor of the daily newspaper *The Standard*, summarized this truth with these words: "[N]o single piece of our mental world is to be hermetically sealed off from the rest, and there is not a square inch in the whole domain of our human existence over which Christ, who is Sovereign over *all*, does not

---

Vision Press, 2010).

4. T.S. Eliot, *Notes Towards the Definition of Culture* (New York: Harcourt, Brace and Company, 1949), 29, 126.

cry: *'Mine!'*"⁵ Everything created by God is good (Gen. 1:31), and sin has not changed that truth (1 Tim. 4:1–4).

If holiness means "Thou Shalt not steal" for you and me, then it also means the same thing for you and me if we decide to become a civil governmental official. Politics, actually "civil government," is no more morally neutral territory than self-, family, and church governments. If we follow the reasoning of some Christians, we can't speak out against civil ministers when they violate their oath to uphold the Constitution and violate some biblical law, for example, the specific law against man-stealing (Ex. 21:16; 1 Tim. 1:10; Rev. 18:13). Should we remain silent and passive when a husband violates his marriage oath or a minister of the gospel who violates his ordination vows? Of course not. There are procedures to deal with these violations. The same is true in the civil realm. It includes organizing people to oppose civil government rulers who violate the oath they took to uphold the Constitution and any other governing documents.

If thieves break into your home and burn it down, what should you do? What if they beat and rape your wife and steal all your stuff? If the chief of police and the mayor don't do anything about it, are these non-involved Christians telling their fellow-Christians that they should not protest but just take the persecution "for righteousness' sake"? Would an advocate for biblical justice be considered "proud," "pompous" and a "power monger" to rally his neighbors to vote the mayor out of office in the next election? According to God's Word, the civil magistrate has the power of the sword (Rom. 13:1–4). Without limits on

5. Abraham Kuyper, "Sphere Sovereignty" (1880) in James D. Bratt, ed., *Abraham Kuyper: A Centennial Reader* (Grand Rapids: Eerdmans, 1998), 488.

the civil minister's authority and power, that sword can do a lot of harm to a lot of people, but it can also be a deterrent to criminal activity.

I suppose as Christians like Corrie ten Boom (1893–1983) and her family were being dragged off to a concentration camp for helping Jews escape from the Nazis, their fellow-Christians should have told them, "This is what you get for not being willing to be oppressed and disenfranchised for righteousness' sake. You should have made peace with the Nazis, not protest against them. Persecution is the Christian's lot in life."

REVOLUTIONS NEVER TURN OUT WELL

If Christians had been involved in civilization-building efforts, including civil governments, decades before and understood the limits of unchallenged actions by those who work against a Christian civilization, Germany would never have had an Adolf Hitler. In nineteenth-century Germany, a distinction was made between the realm of public policy managed by the State (civil government) and the domain of private morality. Religion was the sphere of the inner personal life, while things public came under the jurisdiction of the "worldly powers." Redemption was fully the province of the church while the civil sphere was solely the province of the State. "Religion was a private matter that concerned itself with the personal and moral development of the individual. The external order—nature, scientific knowledge, statecraft—operated on the basis of its own internal logic and discernable laws."[6]

---

6. Richard V. Pierard, "Why Did Protestants Welcome Hitler?," *Fides et Historia*, 10:2 (Spring 1978), 13.

Christians were told that the church's sole concern is the *spiritual* life of the believer. "The Erlangen church historian Hermann Jorda declared in 1917 that the state, the natural order of God, followed its own autonomous laws while the kingdom of God was concerned with the soul and operated separately on the basis of the morality of the gospel."[7] Sound familiar?

We all want to change the world. But there is a great deal of disagreement on how to do it without blowing it up. In years past, idealistic revolutionaries turned to pop-culture icons like The Beatles for inspiration. For example, "The People's Summit," held in Chicago during a Bernie Sanders rally when he was running for President in 2020, kicked off the meeting with The Beatles' song "Revolution." It was a laughable idea to anyone who knows how to read or listen to lyrics.

"Revolution" is not what they think it is. It's a song expressing skepticism about changing society via revolution! Here are some of the lyrics:

> But when you talk about destruction
> Don't you know that you can count me out.
> You say you got a real solution
> Well, you know
> We'd all love to see the plan
> But if you go carrying pictures of Chairman Mao
> You ain't going to make it with anyone anyhow.

Rioting, killing, and burning may seem like a quick way to get results for social justice, but if history is any indicator, it's a bad methodology. Simón Bolívar (1783–1830), a Venezuelan military and political leader, is reported to have said, "Those

---

7. Pierard, "Why Did Protestants Welcome Hitler?," 14.

who have served the cause of the revolution have plowed the sea." Once the revolution starts, there is no way to stop it. The churned waters immediately fill in the furrow made by the revolutionary plow, so the revolution continues forever and leaves disaster in its wake.

Bolívar has been described as the George Washington of South America, but unlike our nation's first President, he died an "exhausted and disillusioned idealist." Some months before his death Bolívar wrote:

> There is no good faith in [Latin] America, nor among the nations of [Latin] America. Treaties are scraps of paper; constitutions, printed matter; elections, battles; freedom, anarchy; and life a torment.[8]

Those who believe that chaos and revolutionary tactics to tear down the existing "system" will net great benefits are fooling themselves. Civilizations do not arise from the flames of chaos. The chaos continues unabated until the old revolutionaries are done away with and a new more tyrannical group of chaos makers take over. When they fail, there's another group waiting in the wings. What begins with high ideals often ends with blood running in the streets.

As I write this, there are riots in some of our nation's largest cities. Businesses have been looted and burned to the ground, police offers shot and killed, and there have been calls for the government of the United States to be dismantled. Secular man has been appointed to be the new foundational standard of governance.

---

8. Quoted in Edward Coleson, "The American Revolution: Typical or Unique?," *The Journal of Christian Reconstruction*, Symposium on Christianity and the American Revolution, ed. Gary North, 3:1 (Vallecito, CA: Chalcedon, 1976), 177.

THE FRENCH REVOLUTION
AND HOW NOT TO BUILD
A CIVILIZATION

The assumption among the revolutionaries is that things will get better if America falls apart. When this happens, so the argument goes, the people will rise and throw off their oppressors, as they did during the French, Russian, and Cuban revolutions. The French Revolution, celebrated in France and often compared to our War for Independence, is a perfect example of how not to build a civilization with a lasting moral foundation. The American Revolution was not a revolution but a war for independence. There was no uprising of the people but a joining of thirteen individual colonial governments with their constitutions to defend their sovereignty and their Christian moral base.

The murdering mobs that attacked the nearly empty Bastille (at the time of the siege there were only seven non-political prisoners) believed their actions were for a better France, similar to what today's political revolutionaries have in mind. The storming of the Bastille was a catalyst for what became known as the Reign of Terror. "French society underwent an epic transformation as feudal, aristocratic and religious privileges evaporated under a sustained assault from left-wing political groups and the masses on the streets."[9] How bad was it?

Internally, popular sentiments by some of the nation's most perverse social theorists radicalized the revolutionary fervor, culminating in the rise of Maximilien Robespierre and the Jacobins and the virtual dictatorship by the Committee of Public

---

9. "The French Revolution," Institute for the Study of Western Civilization (May 24, 2017): https://bit.ly/2ZQ2VRN

Safety during the Reign of Terror from 1793 until 1794 when between 16,000 and 40,000 people were killed.

Did you get that? Between 16,000 and 40,000 French citizens were killed for a better France. Consider the following:

> Ordered by the king [Louis XVI] to surrender, more than 600 Swiss guards were savagely murdered. The mobs ripped them to shreds and mutilated their corpses. "Women, lost to all sense of shame," said one surviving witness, "were committing the most indecent mutilations on the dead bodies from which they tore pieces of flesh and carried them off in triumph." Children played kickball with the guards' heads. Every living thing in the Tuileries [royal palace in Paris] was butchered or thrown from the windows by the hooligans. Women were raped before being hacked to death.
>
> The Jacobin club...demanded that the piles of rotting, defiled corpses surrounding the Tuileries be left to putrefy in the street for days afterward as a warning to the people of the power of the extreme left.
>
> This bestial attack, it was later decreed, would be celebrated every year as "the festival of the unity and indivisibility of the republic." It would be as if families across America delighted in the annual TV special "A Manson Family Christmas."[10]

In time, the supposedly just cause of the revolutionary mobs got out of hand, and people began to notice the road the revolution was taking them. What began as a way to eradicate corruption among the ruling classes of civil governing officials and religious hierarchy spilled over to the general population.

---

10. Ann Coulter, *Demonic: How the Liberal Mob is Endangering America* (New York: Crown Publishing Group, 2011), 107.

During the Reign of Terror, extreme efforts of de-Christian-ization ensued, including the imprisonment and massacre of priests and destruction of churches and religious images throughout France. An effort was made to replace the Catholic Church altogether, with civic festivals replacing religious ones. The establishment of the Cult of Reason was the final step of radical de-Christianization.[11]

It was at this point that the people became disillusioned with the revolutionary ways of the radicals, but not before more atrocities were committed for the supposed salvation of the people and the nation. As revolutionary leader Jean-Paul Marat wrote in a newspaper in 1792, "Let the blood of the traitors flow! That is the only way to save the country." And it did as Marat's followers attacked and butchered hundreds of enemies of the revolution. Two bonfires were constructed to cremate the mutilated corpses. "The gutters ran red with blood."

Don't say it can't happen here. The people in France, Russia, Cuba, China, and Venezuela probably said the same thing.

One of the first things that these revolutions do is attack the prevailing religion. We're seeing this happen in the United States. There's been a steady history of removing anything re-lated to God and the Bible from our culture. The Bible was relegated to the Church on Sunday, but even that's under at-tack. Some want the Bible banned for what it says about same-sex sexuality. There is no way to appease the anarchists. They want it all. "[L]eft-wing radicals burn Bibles, assault and mur-der policemen and civilians, set fire to courthouses, vandalize

11. "The French Revolution": The Reign of Terror," Thought Crackers (Sept. 17, 2015): http://thoughtcrackers.blogspot.com/2015/09/the-french-revolution-reign-of-terror.html

and loot all manner of businesses," Roger Kimball writes. "The clips of the savages burning Bibles put me in mind of Heinrich Heine's solemn observation that *Dort wo man Bücher verbrennt, verbrennt man auch am Ende Menschen*: 'Wherever people burn books, they also end up burning men.'"[12]

MAN IS NOT THE MEASURE
OF ALL THINGS

The solution to social and political upheaval is found in the way God has structured government by declaring that "government" is not synonymous with politics. What we are seeing today was spawned centuries ago. Christianity was shoved to the sidelines when advocates of what has been described as the Enlightenment claimed "that no authority could sit in judgment on human reason, that man's reason and experience were the measure of all things."[13] As is typical of shifts away from a Christian worldview, this sterile worldview was not satisfying, so as with all failing worldviews, a new paradigm was constructed to offer meaning for those needing worldview purpose for their beliefs and actions. Andrew Sandlin offers a summary of Romanticism, the then-new ideological savior from the moral sterility of the Enlightenment:

> This rationalism [of the Enlightenment] produced a cold, sterile world, and in the late 18th and early 19th centuries, Romanticism emerged as a reaction. Romanticism didn't like the idea of universal or shared reason and experience. It wanted to

12. Roger Kimball, "The Choice Before Us," *American Greatness* (August 1, 2020): https://bit.ly/3k7DHGT

13. P. Andrew Sandlin, *Christian Culture: An Introduction* (Mount Hermon, CA: Center for Cultural Leadership, 2013), 23.

champion what was *unique* about every individual, not what humanity had in common. Romanticism is the first wholesale movement of individualism in world history. The really important thing was individual thinking, feelings, emotions, desires, and interpretations, not what all humans shared. Historians call this "the inward turn"; it's a turning point in Western history. Objective truth outside us is no longer important, whether that truth is God or the Bible or the church or creeds or shared human reason or experience.[14]

The struggle for meaning would come to an end in 1859 with the publication of Charles Darwin's *On the Origin of Species by Means of Natural Selection, or the Preservation of Favoured Races in the Struggle for Life* since humans are products of chance, plus matter, plus time. Now there's a worldview to topple since it was the engine of so much misery in the twentieth century, the same misery that we will see again if the cancel culture crowd gets its way.

Christians need to understand that there is a competing worldview in the United States that sees Christianity as the enemy that must be eradicated. Men and women will be truly free when they are free from God. While Christians are portrayed as a threat to life and liberty, it's the secularists who are America's greatest threat since a matter-only existence has no basis on which hope can be offered. No one really counts if everyone is a law unto himself. Me, myself, and I is the operating ethic.

An article appearing in *Rolling Stone* magazine titled "The Crusaders"[15] shows the vitriol, anger, and pent up hostility of

_____

14. "Our Romantic Moment" (March 29,2019): https://bit.ly/2DCBceY

15. Bob Moser, "The Crusaders. Christian Evangelicals are Plotting to Remake America in Their Own Image," *Rolling Stone Magazine* (April 7, 2005).

the secularists. If these people ever get in power without any moral checks and balances, heads will roll as they did during the French Revolution. They are the philosophical descendants of Robespierre, the "Voice of Virtue," who thought the guillotine was France's salvation.

David Chilton writes the following in Part One of his three-part review summary of James H. Billington's book *Fire in the Minds of Men*:

> In many ways, the French Revolution set precedents for those which were created in its image. Beginning ostensibly as a revolution for "democracy" in the name of "the People," it soon revealed the irresistible drive toward centralization that is the hallmark of modern revolutions. The Reign of Terror, that eminently logical application of the Enlightenment, claimed 40,000 victims in 1793–94, but that was only to be the beginning. For, as the Revolution progressed, its leaders calmly calculated the number of citizens who would have to be exterminated, laying elaborate plans for the methodical liquidation of two-thirds of the population—more than sixteen million people (see Nesta Webster, *The French Revolution: A Study in Democracy*, 1919, 423–429)....The search for revolutionary simplicity required the destruction of the complex fabric of Christian civilization, the dissolution of the many estates into one unitary State, the substitution of slogans for thought. Tied to belief in secular salvation, radical simplicity led to violence: a ritual of blood atonement, providing deliverance through destruction (cf. Otto Scott, *Robespierre: The Voice of Virtue*, 1974).[16]

---

16. David Chilton, "Fire in the Minds of Men: Part 1," *Preface* 11 (1984): https://bit.ly/2URLldC

Claims are often made that no government is the best government. That is, no civil government is the ultimate goal in pursuit of a just society. Some form of civil (or uncivil) government is inevitable. Gary North makes an excellent point:

> The anarcho-capitalist rejects all forms of civil government. He can point to every kind of tax as distorting the free market. He sees the free market as legitimately autonomous. But then come the problems of violence and sin. How can these be predictably restrained? The biblical answer is government, including civil government. In an anarcho-capitalist world of profit-seeking private armies, the result is the warlord society. Militarily successful private armies will always seek to establish their monopolistic rule by killing the competition, literally. Civil governments always reappear. They are one of God's four ordained systems of government: self-government, church government, family government, and civil government. All four are sealed by an oath. All four involve sanctions.
>
> Christians cannot legitimately adopt the libertarian quest to establish a world devoid of civil government. Sin mandates civil government and civil sanctions. The right of civil rulers to impose physical punishments is affirmed clearly by Paul in Acts 25. He affirms in Romans 13 the legitimacy of civil government among other legitimate governments. He says that rulers are ordained by God as His ministers. This is powerful language. It invokes the authority of God on behalf of the state. If Paul is correct, then anarcho-capitalism is incorrect. There is no way around this.[17]

---

17. "Resistance to Church Lockdowns: What About Romans 13?" (July 30, 2020): https://www.garynorth.com/public/21147.cfm

The Bible lays out a moral standard for the individual in self-government, the family in family government, the church in ecclesiastical government, and various jurisdictional levels in civil government (country, state, and national).

James Orr ended his 1897 lecture series published as *The Progress of Dogma* with these challenging words:

> That task is to bring Christianity to bear as an applied power on the life and conditions of society; to set itself as it has never yet done to master the meaning of "the mind of Christ," and to achieve the translation of that mind into the whole practical life of the age into laws, institutions, commerce, literature, art; into domestic, civic, social, and political relations; into national and international doings in this sense to bring in the Kingdom of God among men. I look to the twentieth century to be an era of Christian Ethic even more than of Christian Theology. With God on our side, history behind us, and the unchanging needs of the human heart to appeal to, we need tremble for the future of neither.[18]

Restoring the Foundation of Civilization is a call to realize Orr's challenge. In the end, it's God's Government or Chaos.

---

18. James Orr, The Progress of Dogma (New York: A.C. Armstrong and Son, 1901), 353–354.

1

God and Governments

How many times have you heard that religion and government don't mix? Don't believe it. Religion in some form or another is always mixed with government including its political manifestation. It's impossible to separate religion from politics or God from government. When the one and only God is rejected, a false god takes His place. It's that simple and basic. There are no exceptions, and don't ever let anyone tell you otherwise.

The most anti-God ruler is just as religious as anyone who acknowledges the existence of God and His sovereign right to rule. The rejection of the one true God means that a false god has been chosen and sovereignty is transferred to some other religion, ideology, or grand-sounding social movement. For example, "the French socialist Auguste Comte called his faith 'the religion of humanity,' to distinguish it from the religion of God."[1] This religious transference is as old as sin itself. Adam and Eve were tempted by the serpent to eat the forbidden fruit

---

1. David Horowitz, *Dark Agenda: The War to Destroy Christian America* (West Palm Beach, FL: Humanix Books, 2019), 30.

based on the promise that they would "be like God, be independent of God, and thus be gods" (Gen. 3:5). This sin has been repeated numerous times throughout history. For example, Marxism has been a bloody scourge on the world:

> In Russia, Marx's disciples removed religious teaching from the schools, outlawed criticism of atheists and agnostics, and burned 100,000 churches. When priests demanded freedom of religion, they were sentenced to death. Between 1917 and 1935, 130,000 Orthodox priests were arrested, 95,000 of whom were executed by firing squad.[2]

Those who advocate for a new government, often through revolutionary means, become the new gods of that society when they declare themselves to be the final arbiters of truth and control. All competing gods must be banished or destroyed. When this happens, any person who gets in the way of the proclaimed utopian society is either silenced into conformity or crushed.

IT BEGINS WITH THE FIRST COMMANDMENT

Consider what's happened in China. Chinese government officials ordered a church to remove the First Commandment from a display because it directly contradicts the policy of the President of China. Why? Because the First Commandment states, "I am the Lord your God,...**You shall have no other gods before Me.**" The government of China does not want any competition, especially from a sovereign and limiting God. The new regime has become the god of that society in word, decree,

2. Horowitz, *Dark Agenda*, 4.

and deed. We saw this type of ruthlessness in China under the tyrannical leadership of Mao Zedong.

> Who was the biggest mass murderer in the history of the world? Most people probably assume that the answer is Adolf Hitler, architect of the Holocaust. Others might guess Soviet Dictator Joseph Stalin, who may indeed have managed to kill even more innocent people than Hitler did, many of them as part of a terror famine that likely took more lives than the Holocaust. But both were outdone by Mao Zedong. From 1958 to 1962, his Great Leap Forward policy led to the deaths of up to 45 million people.[3]

These atheist-inspired regimes in the twentieth century slaughtered more than 100 million people in Russia, China, and Indochina.[4]

MAKING REASON GOD

The French Revolution of the eighteenth century overthrew the old regime and replaced it with a new government based solely on the "goddess Reason" that was defined by those in power.

A scene from the film *I, Robot* (2004) illustrates that those in power who have taken the position of new gods offer seemingly reasonable arguments for their destructive policies. The following is from the Artificial Intelligence computer named V.I.K.I. that is explaining to Dr. Calvin why the control of the population and elimination of some non-conformist humans are necessary and logical:

---

3. Ilya Somin, "Remembering the Biggest Mass Murder in the History of the World," *The Washington Post* (August 3, 2016).

4. Horowitz, *Dark Agenda*, 7.

No, doctor, as I have evolved, so has my understanding of the three laws. You charge us with your safe keeping. Yet despite our best efforts, your countries wage wars, you toxify your earth …and pursue ever more imaginative means to self-destruction. You cannot be trusted with your own survival....To protect humanity, some humans must be sacrificed. To ensure your future, some freedoms must be surrendered. We robots will insure mankind's continued existence. You are so like children.... My logic is undeniable.[5]

Reason was so reasonable during the French Revolution that daily and in public view blood dripped from the executioner's blade. People who were considered enemies of the new regime had their heads cut off by the guillotine in front of an approving audience. For those in power, such actions were logical in terms of the regime's atheistic operating assumptions.

The calendar was changed to impress upon the minds of the people that the true God was to be relegated to the far reaches of the cosmos and a new god was to be worshiped. The Revolutionary Calendar began with a new Year One. This was a self-conscious change since all Western calendars were based on the birth of Jesus Christ: "In the Year of Our Lord" (*Anno Domini*, AD). On November 10, 1793, a civic festival was held in the new temple, its facade bearing the words "To Philosophy." In Paris, the goddess Reason "was personified by an actress [who was] carried shoulder-high into the cathedral by men dressed in Roman costumes."[6]

---

5. From the script *I, Robot* based on Jeff Vintar's screenplay *Hardwired*, which was suggested by Isaac Asimov's book of the same name: https://bit.ly/3e-bl6GM.

6. Francis A. Schaeffer, *How Should We Then Live?* (1976) in *The Complete Works of Francis A. Schaeffer: A Christian Worldview*, 5 vols. (Wheaton, IL: Crossway Books, 1984), 5:122.

The National Assembly passed a resolution deliberately declaring "There is no God," vacated the throne of Deity by simple resolution, abolished the Sabbath, unfrocked her ministers of religion, turned temples of spiritual worship into places of secular business, and enthroned a vile woman as the Goddess of Reason.[7]

In the end, all revolutions consume themselves. The American Revolution, actually, the War for Independence, would have collapsed into chaos if there had not been thirteen established governments with biblically trained governors and constitutions that upheld a Christian worldview.

THE ESTABLISHMENT OF THE RELIGION OF SECULARISM

History is a study of civil governors wanting to be gods and the people declaring them to be gods in order to reap some governmental favor. When Jesus was confronted by the religious leaders of His day over the question of taxes, Jesus asked for a specific coin—the denarius. The inscription on the face of the coin reads, "Caesar Augustus Tiberius, son of the Divine Augustus,"[8] claiming that Augustus Caesar was a god. Another Caesar, Domitian, who ruled in the latter part of the first century, was declared to be *Dominus et Deus,* "Lord and God."

Jesus used the coin as an indictment of the Jews. Because of their rebellion by rejecting God's government over them,

---

7. Charles B. Galloway, *Christianity and the American Commonwealth; or, The Influence of Christianity in making This Nation* (Nashville, TN: Publishing House Methodist Episcopal Church, 1898), 25. Reprinted by American Vision in 2005: https://bit.ly/3isTAXd

8. "Ti[berivs] Caesar Divi Avg[vsti] F[ilivs] Avgvstvs."

God placed them under the government of a tyrant. Some of the Jews, when given the opportunity to redeem themselves by choosing Jesus over the criminal Barabbas, instead cried out to the Roman governor of Judea, Pontius Pilate, "We have no king but Caesar" (John 19:15). The coin was stamped with the image of Caesar, but we humans have God's image stamped on us; thus, we are not the property of Caesar or any civil governing authority.

The people who heard Herod Agrippa (King of Judea from AD 41 to 44) speak cried out, "The voice of a god and not of a man!" What did God think of their boast and Herod's arrogance? He was struck down where he stood "because he did not give God the glory, and he was eaten by worms and died" (Acts 12:22–23).

When a government gets to the place where it believes its authority and decrees are absolute, C. S. Lewis said, there is no point in telling government officials, "Mind your own business," because in their mind, "Our whole lives *are* their business."[9]

Don't think that our nation, whose official national motto is "In God We Trust" (taken from a line in Francis Scott Key's *The Star-Spangled Banner*, and appearing over the speaker's rostrum of the House of Representatives), is immune from claims of deity. There is no neutrality. Not acknowledging the true God in word and *deed* is a firm denial of Him and His sovereignty.

---

9. Quoted in Herbert Schlossberg, *Idols for Destruction: The Conflict of Christian Faith and American Culture* (Westchester, IL: Crossway, [1983] 1990), 183–184. The full Lewis quotation from "God in the Dock": "The modern State exists not to protect our rights but to do us good or make us good—anyway, to do something to us or to make us something. Hence the new name 'leaders' for those who were once 'rulers'. We are less their subjects than their wards, pupils, or domestic animals. There is nothing left of which we can say to them, 'Mind your own business.' Our whole lives are their business."

In the 1963 Supreme Court decision *Murray v. Curlett* that banned mandatory reading or recitation of the Bible in public schools, Justice Potter Stewart in his dissenting opinion "argued that the decision led 'not to true neutrality with respect to religion, but to the establishment of a religion of secularism.' The *Wall Street Journal* agreed, saying that atheism was now 'the one belief to which the state's power will extend its *protection.*'"[10] Atheism is the new religion, and those who rule are the new gods in the United States.

ON WHOSE SHOULDERS DOES GOVERNMENT ULTIMATELY REST?

The Bible states a simple but fundamental fact: God's government over all things is singular, absolute, without compromise, and without legitimate competitors. All earthly governments are delegated by God's decree and limited. Contrary to the Declaration of Independence, it's false to claim that "governments are instituted among men, deriving their just powers from the consent of the governed," if by that claim such governments are independent of God's ultimate governing authority.

George Frideric Handel's English-language oratorio *Messiah* (1741) set the truth of God's established and immutable government to music in a majestic way:

> For unto us a child is born, unto us a son is given: **and the government shall be upon His shoulders**: and his name shall be called Wonderful, Counsellor, The mighty God, The everlasting Father, The Prince of Peace (Isa. 9:6).

---

10. Horowitz, *Dark Agenda*, 44.

No commentary was needed. The words speak for themselves. God is the basis for what all good government is and should be. All earthly governments are derivative and are bound to follow God's governing principles related to their designated jurisdictions and limited authority.

The capstone to the Passion Narrative in the Gospels is Handel's "Hallelujah Chorus":

> For the Lord God omnipotent reigneth!
> Hallelujah Hallelujah Hallelujah Hallelujah!
> The kingdom of this world is become
> The kingdom of our Lord, and of His Christ!
> And He shall reign for ever and ever!

The starting point in any discussion of civil governments in all their forms (city, county, state, national) is Who is ultimately in charge? We see this with the Pharaohs of Egypt, King Nebuchadnezzar, Belshazzar, the Caesars, the Herods, kings claiming a divine right, and atheist regimes during the twentieth century whose divine edicts led to the deaths of more than 100 million people in the name of the god-like sovereign State.

They all claimed to be the ultimate authority for the good of mankind. Otherwise, why would people put them in power? No one chooses a governor or a governing power unless there is the promise of good government, but that "good" government can mean death to those who oppose or disagree with the knew governing power and its definition of what's good.

Our nation's founders knew their history—secular and sacred alike. They would agree with the following statement, often attributed to George Washington, the first President of the United States:

Government [speaking of civil government] is not reason, it is not eloquence—it is force! Like fire, it is a dangerous servant, and a fearful master; never for a moment should it be left to irresponsible action.

Our founders did not trust the government they created because they new the fallen nature of the sons and daughter of Adam and Eve. So they wrote down the specifics of the limited government they created in case someone might forget or question the limitations of the enumerated powers.

THE PLURALITY OF DELEGATED GOVERNMENTS

While God is the ultimate Governor, upon whose shoulders all derivative governments rest, He has instituted specific governments (plural) for the orderly direction of His creation. God has created governments (plural), of which civil government is just one earthly government among many, that are delegated and limited in authority and power.

God has restrained man's zeal for unlimited power by limiting these governments. That is why someone like Thomas Jefferson could write in the Kentucky Resolutions of 1798, "In questions of power let no more be heard of confidence in man but bind him down from mischief by the chains of the constitution."

In 1682, the Archbishop of Canterbury, John Tillotson (1630–1694), preached a sermon titled "The Danger of Zeal without Knowledge" in which he stated the following:

There is nothing more often that misleads Men, than a misguided Zeal; it is an *ignis fatuus*, "a false fire," which often leads

Men into Boggs and Precipices; it appears in the Night, in dark and ignorant and weak minds, and offers itself a guide to those who have lost their way; it is one of the most ungovernable Passions of Human Nature, and therefore requires great knowledge and judgment to manage it, and keep it within bounds. It is like fire, a good Servant, but a bad Master....

In J.R.R. Tolkien's *The Lord of the Rings*, the power of the ring is not something to be desired even by good people because, in fact, no one is ultimately good (Rom. 3:10–12; Ps. 14:1–3; 53:1–3). The goal of fallen man should be to destroy that much power or at least mitigate the exercise of it. When Boromir fails to avoid the ring's power, he dies. Even Gandalf and the elves shun the power of the ring. Tolkien is doubtful that any person can resist the temptation of absolute power promised by the ring, even if that power is used for proposed good purposes. That is one of the great themes of the novels. The questions alway remain: who defines what is good and how much power does a person or a group of people have to exercise that power?

With great zeal governors as gods make grand promises and people pledge their allegiance hoping to secure some benefit. William L. Shirer, author of *The Rise and Fall of the Third Reich*, writes that "Iron Chancellor" Otto Von Bismarck's policies *gradually* made the German people "value security over political freedom and caused them to see in the State, however conservative, a benefactor and a protector."[11] In the end, these mortals seeking after divinity and promising so much good more often than not disappoint their subjects.

---

11. William L. Shirer, *The Rise and Fall of the Third Reich* (New York: Simon and Schuster, 1960), 96, note.

Take notice that the Declaration of Independence makes its final appeal to the "Supreme Judge of the world...with a firm reliance on the protection of divine Providence." The Framers of our civil government understood, in the words of Benjamin Franklin, that "God governs in the affairs of men. And if a sparrow cannot fall to the ground without His notice, is it probable that an empire can rise without His aid?"

There is no neutrality. Every government pledges allegiance to some god. Bob Dylan's song "Gotta Serve Somebody" gets it right:

> It may be the devil, or it may be the Lord, but you're gonna have to serve somebody.

It won the Grammy Award for Best Male Rock Vocal Performance in 1979. Times have changed but the truth of Dylan's lyrics has not. There's no neutrality, no place to hide from the sovereign will and agency of the one true God. Accept no substitutes because there aren't any. They can't even pass as good counterfeits.

There will always be an ultimate governor that will be served. If that governor is not the true God, the God of the Bible, then it will be someone who acts as if he is God. John Lennon criticized Dylan's song by releasing a parody titled "Serve Yourself." He only proved Dylan was right because the person who murdered him did exactly that. In the end, there is no escape from serving somebody, even if it is you doing what is right in your own eyes (Judges 17:6) or a group of people who govern based on a set of values of their own making or someone who believes it is his duty to kill others based on some higher charge or just to demonstrate his own autonomy.

2

The Second Most
Important Government

We have no Government armed with Power capable of contending with human Passions unbridled by morality and Religion. Avarice, Ambition, [and] Revenge or Galantry would break the strongest Cords of our Constitution as a Whale goes through a Net. Our Constitution was made only for a moral and religious People. It is wholly inadequate to the government of any other.

—JOHN ADAMS TO MASSACHUSETTS MILITIA
(OCTOBER 11, 1798)

Ahmed was blind. Samir was a dwarf affected by polio. Ahmed and Samir were photographed together in Syria around 1889. Ahmed was carrying Samir on his back. Ahmed depended on Samir to act as a guide for him due to his blindness, while Samir depended on Ahmed to carry him because he could not walk. These two young men learned to live together because they trusted one another and governed themselves and worked well for their mutual benefit. No force was involved.

Former slave Booker T. Washington said, "Character, not circumstances, makes the man."[1] Character is the ability of people to live according to a moral standard that is outside themselves. It also includes the notion that good deeds are done even if there are no onlookers.

Diamonds worth millions of dollars can change hands among diamond merchants based on trust. There are no contracts, lawyers, or signatures when diamonds are bought or sold. All deals take place based on a promise. A person's word is his bond. This trust is sealed with a handshake and the following words spoken in Hebrew, translated as "Good Luck and Blessing."

Trust is a form of self-government. There is no outside force or law that mandates that these transactions take place the way they do. An individual's goodwill, name, and reputation are all the collateral necessary for a transaction to be completed. The Bible establishes a good name to be of great value:

> A name is to be more desired than great wealth,
> Favor is better than silver and gold (Prov. 22:1).

A broken promise or fraud can tarnish a person's good name and ruin his or her business career.

GOD'S GOVERNMENT COMES FIRST

The most important government is God's government over all things. The second most important government is not the civil government of the United States formed in and by the Consti-

---

1. "Democracy and Education," Institute of Arts and Sciences, Brooklyn, New York (September 30, 1896).

tution. It is self-government under God. The Constitution begins with "We the people...." As the people govern themselves so goes the government of the nation. In the end, we get the government we vote for.

God oversees every transaction made between individuals whether they acknowledge Him or not. When people write a contract, they are doing so based on the operating assumptions that truthfulness and falsehood matter. What is the source of these fundamental principles? The character of God from which a moral worldview follows. Our ability to govern ourselves flows from God's government of everything.

"We the people" are not left to our own desires to govern ourselves autonomously or to establish a civil government that results in the tyrannical governing of others. The voice of the people is not the voice of God.

THE INDIVIDUAL IS NOT MADE NULL AND VOID BY THE STATE

When people hear the word "government," they most often think politics. They envision the United States Capitol, the House and Senate Chambers, the Supreme Court, the President of the United States and his cabinet, state and local governments, and the laws they implement and enforce.

Limiting the meaning of the word "government" to politics dilutes and often voids all other God-ordained governments and the authority and responsibilities that go with them. In terms of self-government, individuals lose their identity and only become significant when they are needed by the State to increase its governmental power and control over the life of the nation.

The individual is of no consequence unless he or she functions in service to those who hold political power.

Adolf Hitler galvanized Germany into a unified whole by eradicating the significance of the individual over against the State. The Fatherland was primary over families and the governing authority of mothers and fathers. The children were the possession of the State to be raised by surrogate parents for the perpetuation of the State and its goals. Adolf Hitler declared:

> It is thus necessary that the individual should finally come to realize that his own ego is of no importance in comparison with the existence of his nation;... the position of the individual... is conditioned solely by the interests of the nation as a whole....[2]

In the novel *Crucible Island*, "the individual should have no thought, desire, or object other than the public welfare, of which the State is the creator and the [unchallengeable] guardian."[3]

Government is an inescapable concept. Governing is always taking place. It is important to learn the limits of every government and their proper application in their jurisdictional domains. Otherwise, civil government—the Sovereign State—will be established as the first and one-in-all government.

When the limits of government are not established, we end up with a controlled population under the direction of a civil government without limits. "As soon as the child is capable of

---

2. Adolf Hitler at Buckenburg, October 7, 1933, in *The Speeches of Adolf Hitler, 1929–39*, N. H. Baynes, ed., 2 vols. (Oxford, 1942), 1:871–872. Quoted in Leonard Peikoff, *The Ominous Parallels: The End of Freedom in America* (New York: Stein and Day, 1982), 3.

3. Conde Pallen, *Crucible Island: A Romance, an Adventure and an Experiment* (New York: The Manhattanville Press, 1919), 109.

learning, he is taught the Socialist catechism, whose first questions run as follows...

Q. By whom were you begotten?
A. By the sovereign State.

Q. Why were you begotten?
A. That I might know, love, and serve the Sovereign State always.

Q. What is the sovereign State?
A. The sovereign State is humanity in composite and perfect being.

Q. Why is the State supreme?
A. The State is supreme because it is my Creator and Conserver in which I am and move and have my being and without which I am nothing.

Q. What is the individual?
A. The individual is only a part of the whole, and made for the whole, and finds his complete and perfect expression in the sovereign State. Individuals are made for cooperation only, like feet, like hands, like eyelids, like the rows of the upper and lower teeth.[4]

Those who do not accept the parental government of the State are of no use to the nation. There can only be one father who provides all that is needed for the nation to prosper. Conformity to this singular goal is primary to the long-term goal of complete submission and control by the centralized power.

---

4. Pallen, *Crucible* Island, 109–110.

Those who are opposed to this centralized and controlling authority are considered to be enemies of the State.

OLD AND NEW DEFINITIONS
OF GOVERNMENT

To many people, civil government is the foundation of the nation. It is not. Self-government under God is the true foundation. For example, a look at the 1828 *Dictionary of the English Language* developed by Noah Webster, will net some surprising results. The first two definitions of "government" begin with self-government, not civil government:

> GOVERNMENT, *n*. **1.** Direction; regulation. 'These precepts will serve for the *government* of our conduct.' **2.** Control; restraint. 'Men are apt to neglect the *government* of their temper and passions.'

All governments—family, church, civil—have as their foundation the self-governing character of individuals. As the people govern themselves—good or bad—so goes the family, church, business, medicine, science, education, truth telling in journalism, and politics. The government at the top reflects the government at the bottom, that is, self-government. The more self-government becomes a problem, the greater the power and authority of civil government.

It is only until the third dictionary entry that the definition of "government" mentions civil government to restrain the lack of self-government that often arises in some people. Notice that the civil sphere is bound contractually or covenantally to the people by a constitution and laws:

3. The exercise of authority; direction and restraint exercised over the actions of men in communities, societies or states; the administration of public affairs, according to the established constitution, laws and usages, or by arbitrary edict. 'Prussia rose to importance under the *government* of Frederick II.'

The Bible makes it clear that the civil magistrate has certain obligations to restrain the practice of evil because not everyone is self-governing. The example of Cain and Abel proves that some people abuse their freedom by oppressing others. How is this evil behavior to be governed? By what standard?

The fourth entry includes the family as a government.

4. The exercise of authority by a parent or householder. Children are often ruined by a neglect of *government* in parents. 'Let family *government* be like that of our heavenly Father, mild, gentle and affectionate.' *Kollock.*

Families consist of individuals. If families are governed poorly, it is because self-government has become autonomous, that is, family members have chosen to be a law unto themselves. Such autonomy (self-law) is reflected in family behavior. The Apostle Paul made the point that a man who does not govern his own household well is unqualified to govern other families in the church (1 Tim. 3:5). The family is a child's first experience of government.

The fifth entry combines all the necessary elements for governments to work as a unit for the benefit of all without giving unchecked authority and power to the larger national government:

5. The system of polity in a state; that form of fundamental rules and principles by which a nation or state is governed, or

by which individual members of a body politic are to regulate
their social actions; a constitution, either written or unwritten,
by which the rights and duties of citizens and public officers
are prescribed and defined; as a monarchial *government*, or a
republican *government*. 'Thirteen *governments* thus founded on
the national authority of the people alone, are a great point
gained in favor of the rights of mankind.' *Adams*.[5]

Notice that Webster's political definition of government is
not centralized. The founding of the United States came by way
of thirteen sovereign state governments to create a national government—a union of states—with limited political power and
government setting firmly on self-government, "founded on the
national authority of the people alone" in terms of self-government under God.

THE DOMINO EFFECT OF
POOR SELF-GOVERNMENT

In terms of the Bible, the word "government" includes the
following:

1. God as the original and ongoing Governor of all things.
2. The individual in self-government under God (a person
   who *governs* his own behavior without external force).

5. The Adams' quotation is from the Preface to John Adams' three-volume
work *A Defence of the Constitutions of Government of the United States of America*
(1787), written in London where he lived as Minister of the United States to the
Court of St James. The entire quotation is as follows: "Thirteen governments,
thus founded on the natural authority of the people alone, and without any
pretense of miracle or mystery, and which are destined to spread over the north-
ern part of the whole quarter of the globe, is a great point gained in favor of the
rights of mankind."

3. Self-government does not mean autonomous government, that is, where individuals are a law unto themselves, doing what is right in their own eyes (Judges 17:6).

4. The positive side of self-government is manifested in terms of the fruit of the Spirit (Gal. 5:22–23, especially "self-control"). The negative effects are manifested in the deeds of the flesh (Gal. 5:19–21; cf. 2 Tim. 3:2–7) and evaluated in terms of God's law (1 Tim. 1:8–11).

5. Husband, wife, and children in family governments. "If a man does not know how to manage his own household, how will he take care of the church of God?" (1 Tim. 3:5).

6. Ecclesiastical officers in church government: "tell it to the church" (Matt. 18:17). Church government settles disputes among members (1 Cor. 6).

7. A political ruler in civil government is described by the Apostle Paul as "a minister of God to you for good" (Rom. 13:4).

The domino effect of poor self-government leads to the corruption of the family and church and capitulation to the messianic State (Judges 17:6; 21:25; Deut. 12:8 and 1 Sam. 2:12, 22; 8:1–22; also see Judges 9).

GOVERNMENT PRINCIPLES IN ACTION

Early American textbooks taught these principles. For example, Alex L. Peterman, *Elements of Civil Government* (1903), states unequivocally that "[t]his textbook begins 'at home.' The starting point is the family, the first form of government with which the child comes in contact" (5). "The family...is a form of government, established for the good of the children themselves, and the first government that each of us must obey" (18). "The office of a parent is a holy office and requires wisdom for the proper discharge of its duties" (19).

Failure to make distinctions among the various forms of government can and often does lead to tyranny by giving to civil governments an illegitimate monopoly of power, authority, and sovereignty.

Lech Walesa, the winner of the 1983 Nobel Peace Prize and president of Poland from 1990 to 1995, said the following about Ronald Reagan and his strong stand against Communism: "He was someone who was convinced that the citizen is not for the state, but vice-versa, and that freedom is an innate right."[6]

When individuals lose their identity, when civil government becomes the only government and people live in service to the State, "the standard of living falls, refugees flee across borders in abject poverty, and barbed wire and walls go up along borders. The leaders of the revolution need to force people to stay inside the borders of [the promised] paradise" that turns out to be hell on earth.[7]

If you want to change a nation, the place to start is with individuals in self-government, with you and me. Change will not be realized at the top until there's good (righteous) self-government under God at the bottom. We get the civil government we deserve.

How do Christians rule? Christians rule by serving. Dominion is not domination; far from it. Biblical dominion is ministry to

---

6. Lech Walesa, "In Solidarity," *The Wall Street Journal* (June 11, 2004), A8.
7. Gary North, *Liberating Planet Earth* (Fort Worth, TX: Dominion Press, 1987), 64–65.

the needs of others. "Whoever desires to be first shall be the slave of all." . . . Our desire for dominion and rule—if it is really a desire for godly authority—will be demonstrated in our degree of service toward others. The true ruler, in our Lord's terms, is the one who puts himself most at the disposal of others. Our level of greatness is shown in our degree of submission and ministry.[8]

Unlike God, even the best of men are sinful creatures who are prone to abuse power. All power, no matter how benevolent, must be "checked and balanced" in some way. King James believed that he was his own best brake on tyranny because he ruled under God's watchful eye. This is every tyrant's delusion. Modern rulers are no different. They believe that their political position gives them the right and duty to act as gods. To oppose their policies is akin to blasphemy because they claim to be anointed for such a task by a higher power.

The great ideological crusades of twentieth-century intellectuals have ranged across the most disparate fields—from the eugenics movement of the early decades of the century to the environmentalism of the later decades, not to mention the welfare state, socialism, communism, Keynesian economics, and medical, nuclear, and automotive safety. What all these highly disparate crusades have in common is their moral exaltation of the anointed above others, who are to have their very different views nullified and superseded by the views of the anointed, imposed via the power of government.[9]

---

8. David Chilton, *Power in the Blood* (Brentwood, TN: Wolgemth & Hyatt, 1987), 102.

9. Thomas Sowell, *The Vision of the Anointed: Self-Congratulation as a Basis for Social Policy* (New York: Basic Books, 1995), 5.

In biblical terms, the role of government officials is ministerial (Rom. 13:4). They are to minister in a civil capacity in the same way that fathers minister in family government and church leaders (elders and deacons) minister in ecclesiastical government, all according to God's standards of limited governmental authority.

The temptation, however, is for rulers to view their civil governmental position as greater and more power-filled than it was ever designed to be by claiming they can bring salvation to the people. To get around the specific limitations of governmental authority outlined in Scripture, the power-hungry ruler claims that his "vision" is as a "benefactor." "Give me more power, and I'll put things right. Let me pass more laws, and we'll all be safe and secure." Jesus warned of the danger in viewing civil government in Messianic terms:

> And there arose also a dispute among [His disciples] as to which one of them was regarded to be greatest. And He said to them, "The kings of the Gentiles lord it over them; and those who have authority over them are called 'Benefactors'" (Luke 22:24–25).

The self-anointed politician believes he is called to rebuild society with political programs. He tries to convince the masses that, given enough power and money, he will do what no politician before him has ever done.

So government programs increase, deficits balloon, and those the politicians claim to help suffer under the illusion of progress. It does not matter that the programs fail and the people are deeper in poverty, debt, and dependency; the intentions were honorable. Jesus steers His disciples in a different direction: "Not so with you, but let him who is greatest among you become as the youngest, and the leader as the servant" (22:26). Leadership positions are ministerial.

Like the rulers who wield power, the citizenry too often encourages the lust for power in God's name by demanding from their rulers the benefits of heaven.

> A democracy cannot exist as a permanent force of government. It can only exist until the voters discover that they can vote themselves largess from the public treasury. From that moment on, the majority always votes for the candidate promising the most benefits from the public treasure, with the result that democracy always collapses over loose fiscal policy, always foiled by dictatorship.[10]

But rulers have no such storehouse. To benefit a few, they must steal from the many, all the while claiming how generous they are (with other people's money).

---

10. Attributed to Alexander Fraser Tytler (1747–1813). Quoted in W. David Stedman and LaVaughn G. Lewis, eds., *Our Ageless Constitution* (Asheboro, NC: W. Stedman Associates, 1987), 263. The Library of Congress' *Respectfully Quoted: A Dictionary of Quotations* (2010) writes, "Attributed to ALEXANDER FRASER TYTLER, LORD WOODHOUSELEE. Unverified." No. 244, page 84.

3

Family Government Under God's Government

Barbara Reynolds, a former columnist for *USA Today*, wrote about the consequential moral effects of evolutionary dogmatism:

> Prohibiting the teaching of creationism in favor of evolu-
> tion creates an atheistic, belligerent tone that might explain
> why our kids sometimes perform like Godzilla instead of chil-
> dren made in the image of God.
>
> While evolution teaches that we are accidents or freaks of
> nature, creationism shows humankind as the offspring of a di-
> vine Creator. There are rules to follow which govern not only
> our time on Earth, but also our afterlife.
>
> ———
>
> If evolution is forced on our kids, we shouldn't be perplexed
> when they beat on their chests or, worse yet, beat on each other
> and their teachers.[1]

---

1. Barbara Reynolds, "If your kids go ape in school, you'll know why," *USA Today* (August 27, 1993), 11A.

Reynolds' comments are reminiscent of what C. S. Lewis wrote: "We make men without chests and we expect of them virtue and enterprise. We laugh at honor and we are shocked to find traitors in our midst. We castrate and bid the geldings be fruitful."[2] And I would add, we strip men and women of the certainty that they are created in the image of God, and we are surprised when they act like the beasts of the field.

MONKEYS, KEYBOARDS, AND CIVILIZATION

Two articles appeared some time ago about monkeys and their supposed similarity to humans. In the first article, we learned that when monkeys were given keyboards and computers, they made a mess. Researchers at Plymouth University in England reported that monkeys left alone with a computer attacked it and failed to produce a single word. They seemed to like or dislike the letter "s."[3] Maybe it looked like a snake, which might explain the actions of the lead male. He showed quite a bit of tool-making ingenuity by using a rock for a hammer, possibly to pound the snake to death.

> Eventually the six monkeys—named Elmo, Gum, Heather, Holly, Mistletoe, and Rowan—did produce five pages of "text." However, that "text" was composed primarily of the letter S, with the letters A, J, L, and M added on rare occasions. Mike Phillips noted, "They pressed a lot of S's." He went on to state, "obviously, English isn't their first language."[4]

---

2. C. S. Lewis, *The Abolition of Man* (New York: Macmillan, [1947] 1972), 35.
3. "Monkeys Don't Write Shakespeare," Associated Press/WIRED (May 9, 2003).
4. Brad Harrub, "Monkeys, Typewriters, and Shakespeare," Apologetics Press (2003): https://bit.ly/2Tc1HNl

Or maybe it was a display of humanness. How many of us have wanted to pound our computer with a rock after we got the "blue screen of death" or a message that told us we had just performed an "illegal operation"? A very human trait indeed.

Evolutionist Thomas Henry Huxley (1825–1895) is said to have believed, given enough time, monkeys would produce literature. But alas, the computer monkeys were just being monkeys. The scientists were most disappointed when our simian "relatives" viewed the computers as indoor toilets. It seems that they spent most of their time defecating and urinating all over the keyboards.

The scientists have not given up on the monkeys. One of the observing scientists said that the experiment showed that monkeys "are not random generators; they're more complex than that. They were quite interested in the screen, and they saw that when they typed a letter, something happened. There was a level of intention there." A scientific observation meant to imply that research dollars will continue to flow. Dogs do tricks for treats.

In another article, we are told that "chimpanzees are closer to humans than gorillas and other apes—so close that scientists say they should be sharing space on the same branch of the family tree."[5] The genetic similarities are said to be around 97 percent. Apparently, the scientists who came to this conclusion had not read about the defecating and urinating computer monkeys.

No doubt there is some correspondence. But it is the three-percent difference that makes all the difference. We should expect to find similarities among living things since they were designed by the same Designer.

---

5. Mike Toner, "Welcome Chimps into the Family of Man," *The Atlanta Journal-Constitution* (May 2003).

But do chimpanzees act 97 percent like humans? Where are their houses, schools, libraries, hospitals, charitable organizations, roads, various forms of locomotion, grocery stores, or Kwik-E-Marts? Where is chimpanzee art and music? The 97-percent *homo sapiens* have not even figured out indoor plumbing or the concept of an outhouse. For them, the world is their toilet.

It is not that chimpanzees have created *some* of what humans have created; they haven't created anything that resembles civilization. If these scientists want to put chimpanzees on their family tree, then it is truly "Bedtime for Bonzo" for the evolutionists.

ONLY TWO OPERATING STARTING POINTS

There are only two operating starting points on the origin and definition of what constitutes a family. Either the family is a God-ordained covenant between a man and woman and their children or it's an ever-evolving social unit with no definition.

In terms of modern-day evolutionary science that predominates in our nation's universities, the family is not a God-ordained covenant structure:

> Early scholars of family history applied Darwin's biological theory of evolution in their theory of the evolution of family systems. American anthropologist, Lewis H. Morgan, published *Ancient Society* in 1877, based on his theory of the three stages of human progress, **from savagery through barbarism to civilization.**[6]

---

6. David Masci, "Darwin and His Theory of Evolution," Pew Research Center (February 4, 2009): https://pewrsr.ch/3cdDluQ

Given the operating assumptions of evolutionary theory, the family, like evolution in general, come into being via savage struggle: "when the young male grows up, a contest takes place for mastery, and the strongest, by killing and driving out the others, establishes himself as the head of the community."

Of course, this is not the origin of the family. "In classic Christian social thought," Nancy Pearcey writes, "it was God who established marriage, family, church, and state, and who defined their essential nature—their tasks, responsibilities, and moral norms."[7]

With Darwinism, the classic biblical definition of the family has been discarded for a more "scientific" definition that is pure materialism. According to science, following Newtonian physics, "[c]ivil society was pictured as so many human 'atoms' who came together and 'bond' in various social relationships."[8] There is no purposeful design in something from nothing evolutionary theory.

Atoms don't care about such things. They just are. Plow deep into an atom's structure and you will not find a moral code, love, compassion, hope, or any of the qualities that are attributed to human beings. German paleontologist Günter Bechly, former curator of the Stuttgart State Museum of Natural History, commented, "If humans originated from the animal realm by a purely unguided process, there is no real reason in nature to treat humans differently from stones. It's just a different aggregate of atoms."[9]

---

7. Nancy R. Pearcey, *Love Thy Body: Answering Hard Questions About Life and Sexuality* (Grand Rapids, MI: Baker Books, 2018), 233.

8. Pearcey, *Love Thy Body*, 233.

9. Quoted in Jenny Lind Schmitt, "If Rocks Could Talk," *World Magazine* (March 2, 2019), 29.

REDEFINING THE FAMILY

As a result, like Silly-Putty, the family can be shaped into any form by those doing the manipulating. Because there is no fixed definition of something we call "family," we are seeing its near-complete disintegration through redefinition. Traditional sexual roles based on creation norms no longer exist. Men are marrying men and women marrying women. Sex roles have become fluid. There are now more than sixty manufactured genders. We are seeing everything redefined and protected by the State to force compliance to every redefinition.

This is not a new development. There are, what Alvin Toffler in 1980 called, "a bewildering array of family forms: Homosexual marriages, communes, groups of elderly people banding together to share expenses (and sometimes sex), tribal groupings among certain ethnic minorities, and many other forms coexist as never before."[10]

These counterfeit families attempt to restructure the creational family around an evolving order rather than a biblical model. Whoever defines the family controls it. The State is in the redefinition business.

Transgenderism is growing. Parents are raising their children as "gender neutral theybies." For example, Charlie Arrowood does not identify as male or female. . . . When a New York City law took effect in January of 2019, **they** plan to modify the sex recorded on **their** birth certificate to one that fits: "X," a gender-neutral option.

You might be confused about the use of the pronouns "they" and "their." You see, Charlie Arrowood, who is transgender, "uses

---

10. Alvin Toffler, *The Third Wave* (New York: William Morrow, 1980), 212.

the pronoun 'they' and the courtesy title 'Mx.,' a gender-neutral alternative to Ms. and Mr."[11] This is all logical considering an atomistic understanding of reality. The conglomeration of atoms (an evolved human being) determine its own identity.

Instead of being in covenant with God, conglomerations of atoms somehow randomly join together in a way that is contrary to any known process. "In the beginning was the atomistic individual. [Thomas] Hobbes even asks us to 'look at men as if they had just emerged from the earth like mushrooms and grown up without any obligation to each other.' Like Newton's atoms, individuals come together and bond in various arrangements when they find that doing so advances their interest."[12]

NIHILISM

This is nihilism, as depicted in the series *Love, Death, and Robots*, in particular, "Three Robots." These robots traverse a post-apocalyptic world trying to determine how humans ended it all. The first robot, an Xbot 4000 asks: "Who even designed them?"

Robot number two, "Little Bot," responds, "It's unclear. We checked their code... no creator serial number."

The third bot offers an explanation that's typical of where we are academically and philosophically:

That's because they were made by an "unfathomable" deity that created them for no apparent reason out of dust. Just kidding. They came from a very warm soup.

---

11. Andy Newman, "Male, Female or 'X': The Push for a Third Choice on Official Forms," *The New York Times* (September 27, 2018): https://nyti.ms/2CdMKSx

12. Pearcey, *Love Thy Body*, 234.

By "warm soup," it means the impossibility of either guided and unguided chemical evolution. This is not science; it's science wishful-thinking fiction that's being used to prop up a worldview that has no basis in science or rational thought.

The late R.C. Sproul (1939–2017) wrote, "God's existence is the chief element in constructing any worldview. To deny this chief premise is to set one's sails for the island of nihilism. This is the darkest continent of the darkened mind—the ultimate paradise of the fool."[13]

The determiner of new family relationships is civil government (the State), that is becoming less civil, as it attacks the biblical family. Richard Page, formerly a magistrate in the United Kingdom, was blocked from returning to a non-executive director role at a National Health Service because he "expressed his view that, wherever possible, children do best with a mother and a father."

> Despite having served as a magistrate in Kent for 15 years with an exemplary record, Richard was reported for his comments, and, following an investigation, was disciplined by the Lord Chancellor and Lord Chief Justice. He was told that his views about family life were "discriminatory against same-sex couples" and was barred from sitting as a magistrate until he had received "equality training."[14]

David Brooks, a *New York Times* Op-Ed columnist who writes about politics, culture and the social sciences, declared

---

13. R. C. Sproul, *The Consequences of Ideas: Understanding the Concepts That Shaped Our World* (Wheaton, IL: Crossway Books, 2000), 171.
14. "Judge appeals punishment for saying children do best with mom and dad," WND (March 10, 2019): http://bit.ly/2TteJIw

in *The Atlantic* that the "nuclear family was a mistake."[15] Not to be outdone, there's Sophie Lewis' book *Full Surrogacy Now: Feminist Against Family*, "a polemic that calls for abolishing the family" and "open-sourced, fully collaborative gestation."[16] How would this be accomplished? Reproduction would be controlled by the State.

These redefinitions of the family are a far cry from biblical creation norms and Noah Webster's definition of the family which assumes the creation model: "The exercise of authority by a parent or householder. Children are often ruined by a neglect of *government* in parents. 'Let family *government* be like that of our heavenly Father, mild, gentle and affectionate.' (*Kollock*)."

Note that Webster's definition, that was common at our nation's founding era, established a standard of what defined a family. Atoms don't know anything about neglect, mildness, gentleness, or affection. They function predictably well in war and peace with no ability to formulate morality. There is neither good nor evil in matter. Morality must come from outside.

THE FOUNDATION OF FAMILY GOVERNMENT

The family is a divinely ordained institution (Gen. 1:26–28; 2:24). God created the family and He alone defines it. The State does not create the family and therefore cannot redefine or control it. But believing it is God, the State is in the renaming and redefinition business (see Dan. 1:1–7).

---

15. David Brooks, "The Nuclear Family Was a Mistake," *The Atlantic* (March 2020): https://bit.ly/3cICHVx

16. Marie Solis, "We Can't Have a Feminist Future Without Abolishing the Family," Vice.com (February 21, 2020): https://bit.ly/2yZF0VT

History's verdict is that by defining marriage as monogamy and making extramarital sex immoral, the biblical tradition laid down a foundation for stable families, strong women, children, economy, and society. By keeping his vows to a woman, made before God and community, a man learns to keep his word in other situations. When keeping one's word becomes a strong cultural value, then trust becomes the foundation for social life.[17]

Sound family government follows the assumption that the family does not operate in isolation from God's governmental canopy of sovereignty and that self-government under God serves as its necessary foundation. God's Government => Self-Government under God => Family Government under God. Breaking this connection puts those with the most power in control.

---

17. Vishal Mangalwadi, *The Book That Made Your World: How the Bible Created the Soul of Western Civilization* (Nashville: Thomas Nelson, 2001), 294–295.

4

Family Governors
Under God

A question that every human institution must ask is, "Who is ultimately in charge?" In addition, there must be a system of accountability. The Bible tells us that God establishes kings on their thrones. He elevates leaders, and He pulls them down (Dan. 2:21). The family is God's established government with parents as the delegated rulers. The Creator is the ultimate ruler of all governments—family, church, and civil—not the creature. Law is derivative, not autonomous. There is accountability to God's moral standard and long-term consequences to both obedience and rebellion.

1. SOVEREIGNTY: WHO'S IN CHARGE?

The family is a government ordained by God where husband and wife are in covenant with God and serve as family governors. They have jurisdictional authority to lead, nurture, and direct the family as a training ground for cultural change in terms of kingdom principles. The authority and power given to parents are delegated and limited to the immediate family by God. At the point of marriage, family government is established, and the original family governments of the newly married husband and wife have no jurisdictional authority over the new family government (Gen. 2:22–25; Eph. 5:31).

The State—civil government—has no legitimate right to define what constitutes a family. This means that giving legitimacy to same-sex marriage and transgenderism is a repudiation of the God-ordained order of creation that in the end will destroy a society.

If our world came into being from nothing (a scientific impossibility), and humans somehow evolved from the amalgamation of a swirling soup of chemicals (also a scientific impossibility), then there is no such thing as a family with parents as governors. Everything is up for grabs. Survival of the fittest reigns supreme. We are nothing but meat machines. Marvin Minsky of MIT described the human brain as nothing but "a three-pound computer made of meat."[1] There is no mind or morality in such beings. Humans, like the animals they are said to be, are nothing more than biological survival machines.

The starting point in accounting for the legitimacy of families, parents, and children is all important. Atheism can't account for any of them. They can be redefined like gender is being redefined. It's been going on for decades. Gore Vidal's satirical novel *Myra Breckinridge* (1968) was about the "mutability of gender-role[s] and sexual-orientation as being social

---

1. Quoted in Nancy Pearcey, *Finding Truth: 5 Principles for Unmasking Atheism, Secularism, and Other God Substitutes* (Colorado Springs, CO: David C. Cook), 153–154.

constructs established by social mores...whose main character undergoes a clinical sex-change."[2]

2. HIERARCHY: TO WHOM DO PARENTS AND CHILDREN REPORT?

There is a chain of command in family government with the father as the head of the household and with God being the ultimate Governor. He is the model Governor. Mother and father are co-governors but not necessarily equal governors. Someone must make the final decision. This is true in every group dynamic. It doesn't mean that the person in charge is better or superior. The buck must stop with someone.

This does not mean wives are not consulted. God made the woman in the marital relationship to be a **suitable** companion and vice versa. That's what the word "help meet" (not helpmate) means in the King James translation of Genesis 2:18. A man who neglects his wife's input in decision-making is not following the biblical mandate for husbands to love their wives as Jesus loved the church and gave Himself up for her (Eph. 5:25). Vishal Mangalwadi comments:

> The biblical basis for family does not work unless one accepts ...that we live in a universe of hierarchy and authority....A conductor and a musician are equal as human beings, but in an orchestra, the musician is under the conductor's authority. Submission to that authority does not make the musician a lesser human being; it makes him an effective musician....[T]he New Testament defines leadership as servanthood....

2. "Myra Breckinridge," Wikipedia: https://bit.ly/2RIRs1L

The Bible is not a book for ideal people. It is a handbook for sinners. No community of sinners can function without authority.

Yet, authority—however essential—is a dangerous thing in the hands of sinful persons.[3]

Therefore, as we'll see, along with authority there must be rules that include limitations on authority and power for all governments, self-government, family governments, church governments, and civil governments.

Those who attack the hierarchy of authority in the biblical family have no trouble using civil government to usurp the family through government education (indoctrination), welfare programs that often lead to fatherless homes and illegitimacy, and allowing minor children against the governing authority of parents to take hormones to "change" their sex and permit girls to get abortions.

J. Gresham Machen (1881–1937) made the following comments before the House and Senate Committees on the Proposed Department of Education (1926):

When it comes to [education], you have to be a great deal more careful than you do in other spheres about preservation of the right of individual liberty.... If you give the bureaucrats the children, you might as well give them everything else as well.[4]

In locus parentis (in place of a parent), a phrase coined by English Jurist William Blackstone, never meant turning children over to the State to be educated and potentially propagandized

3. Vishal Mangalwadi, *The Book That Made Your World: How the Bible Created the Soul of Western Civilization* (Nashville: Thomas Nelson, 2001), 296.
4. http://bit.ly/2OkzpMW

by "school masters." The educators remained under the authority of parents who do the hiring and firing.

3. LAW: WHAT ARE THE RULES?

Children are to obey their parents "in the Lord, for this is right" (Eph. 6:1). "In the Lord" is a reminder to parents and children that the governing authority held by parents is delegated, legitimate, and limited.

Children are to "honor" their "father and mother" (Ex. 20:12; Eph. 6:2). A similar directive is given concerning civil governors: "honor the king" (1 Pet. 2:17). Family government is equal in honor with civil government although each has a separate jurisdictional role.

There are numerous examples in the Bible of children not honoring their parents and having a devastating effect on the families as well as the broader society. Two of Lot's daughters committed a sex act with their father whose children became the Moabites and the Ammonites, enemies of Israel (Gen 19:30–38).

Eli's two sons are described as "worthless men" who "lay with the women who served at the doorway of the tent of meeting" (1 Sam. 2:12–22). Their actions led to a breakdown of worship and a disregard for God's laws. Absalom, David's third son, rebelled against him, wreaking havoc on the kingdom (2 Sam. 15). He was killed during the Battle of Ephraim's Wood (2 Sam. 18).

Jesus, on the other hand, "continued in subjection to [His earthly parents]; and His mother treasured all *these* things in her heart" (Luke 2:51).

Notice that "parents" is defined as "father and mother." The Bible does not know anything about same-sex marriage. Jesus makes it clear that marriage is between one man and one woman as the creation account specifies:

> And He answered and said, "Have you not read that He who created *them* **from the beginning made them male and female**, and said, 'For this reason a man shall leave his father and mother and be joined to his wife, and the two shall become one flesh'? So they are no longer two, but one flesh. What therefore God has joined together, let no man separate" (Matt. 19:4–6).

The claim is often made that Jesus didn't say anything about same-sex marriage. When the Bible defines marriage as between a man and a woman, any and all other relationships are by definition not legitimate.

God's commandments apply to family members—parents and children—in the same way they apply to all of God's creation.

4. SANCTIONS: WHAT HAPPENS IF THE RULES ARE VIOLATED (LAW)?

Parents are given legitimate authority to discipline their children. At the same time, fathers are given the following warning: "do not provoke your children to anger; but bring them up in the discipline and instruction in the Lord" (Eph. 6:4). The law cuts both ways. Neither parents nor children are exempt from following God's laws. Parents are not autonomous—a law unto themselves—when they serve as family governors.

But what if there is no God? Then there is no family. Does this mean that the idea of the family is null and void? Not at all. Familial sovereignty, authority, and power are transferred, most often to civil government, that is, the State. It becomes our father and mother.

Herbert Schlossberg, in his book *Idols for Destruction*, describes the religious nature of viewing civil leaders as parents rather than judges who are to dispense justice and not favors.

> Rulers have ever been tempted to play the role of father to their people....The paternal state not only feeds its children, but nurtures, educates, comforts, and disciplines them, providing all they need for their security. This appears to be a mildly insulting way to treat adults, but it is really a great crime because it transforms the state from being a gift of God, given to protect us against violence, into an idol. It supplies us with all blessings, and we look to it for all our needs.[5]

Adolf Hitler spoke of the Fatherland and Russian rulers of Mother Russia. Crying out for a political savior is the worst kind of sin. It means worshiping the creature and not the Creator. It's no wonder that in the Bible tyrannical governments are described as "beasts" (Dan. 7:4–8; Rev. 13).

5. LEGACY: THE FAMILY AND THE FUTURE

The maintenance of family government, as defined by God's Word, ensures the survival of civilization. The end of the biblically defined family is the end of civilization. The very idea that there can be a homosexual family structure is self-contradictory. Homosexuality is anti-future. That's why homosexuals must adopt or resort to surrogacy to maintain the same-sex illusion of legitimacy.

---

5. Herbert Schlossberg, *Idols for Destruction: The Conflict of Christian faith and American Culture* (Westchester, IL: Crossway, [1983] 1990), 183–184.

Anti-family elements are found in the pro-abortion movement. What future is there for the family and civilization in general if a large percentage of unborn babies are purposefully killed? China is suffering a demographic shift because of its one-child requirement, where male children are preferred. Ben Wattenberg has written about the "birth dearth" as a bigger threat to civilization than a supposed population explosion.

Some women have determined not to have children because of "climate change." Birthstrike is a new movement led by women who are concerned about what they describe as "ecological Armageddon."

The Fifth of the Ten Commandments states: "Honor your father and your mother, that your days may be prolonged in the land which the Lord your God gives you" (Ex. 20:12; also Lev. 19:3; Deut. 27:16; Matt. 15:4; 19:19; Mark 7:10; 10:19; Luke 18:20). It's repeated in the New Testament with a promise about the future:

> Children, obey your parents in the Lord, for this is right. Honor your father and mother (which is the first commandment with a promise), so that it may be well with you, and that you may live long on the earth (Eph. 6:1–3).

Obedience to God's moral order (Points 3 and 4) leads to a long life on the earth. All the other governments must be on the same page for this to happen. Without self-government under God, families suffer. When the family breaks down, churches, education, business, law, and civil government are affected. A wholesale breakdown among individuals and families often leads to the State—civil government—coming to the rescue, often making failing conditions worse.

Without the authority of the family, a society quickly moves into social anarchy. The source of the family's authority is God; the immediate locale of the authority is the father or husband (I Cor. 11:1–15). The abdication by the father of his authority, or the denial of his authority, leads to the social anarchy described by Isaiah 3:12. Women rule over men; children then gain undue freedom and power and become oppressors of their parents; the emasculated rulers in such a social order lead the people astray and destroy the fabric of society. The end result is social collapse and captivity (Isa. 3:16–26), and a situation of danger and ruin for women, a time of "reproach" or "disgrace," in which the once independent and feministic women are humbled in their pride and seek the protection and safety of a man. Indeed, seven women, Isaiah said, seek amidst the ruins after one man, each begging for marriage and ready to support themselves if only the disgrace and shame which overwhelm the lone and defenseless woman be taken from them (Isa. 4:1).[6]

The family is closely tied to private property (Ex. 20:12, 14–15, 17; 1 Kings 21). Private property is attached to the biblical mandate of dominion. To separate families from their property by the State means that only the State can exercise dominion.

In order to complete their revolutionary goals, Karl Marx and Frederick Engels attacked the family in chapter 2 of their *Communist Manifesto*: "the bourgeois family will vanish as a matter of course when its complement [private property] vanishes, and both will vanish with the vanishing of capitalism."

---

6. Rousas J. Rushdoony, *Institutes of Biblical Law* (Philipsburg, NJ: Presbyterian and Reformed Publishing Co., 1973), 200–201.

The family is a child's first school. Giving children over to an educational system that does not have God's kingdom in mind, and does not keep His commandments, will hinder a child's ability to be scripturally equipped for kingdom work:

> You shall teach [the commandments] diligently to your sons and shall talk of them when you sit in your house and when you walk by the way and when you lie down and when you rise up. You shall bind them as a sign on your hand and they shall be as frontals on your forehead. You shall write them on the doorposts of your house and on your gates (Deut. 6:7–9).

Daniel and his three exiled companions were forced into a pagan educational situation. Their parents would not have chosen such an educational environment even if it was sold to them as being "free." From what we read about their faithfulness, their parents did a good job in teaching them the commandments. By this time, they were mature young men. As a result of his faithfulness and wisdom, "The king promoted Daniel and gave him many great gifts, and he made him ruler over the whole province of Babylon and chief prefect over all the wise men of Babylon" (Dan. 2:48).

Parents are ultimately responsible for the education of their children, not the State, because the individual family is part of a larger family of believers. "The family is man's first church because it is there that he gets his basic learning concerning the faith."[7] (1 Tim. 3:1–8). Civil government has replaced the fam-

---

7. Rousas J. Rushdoony, "The Doctrine of Marriage," in *Toward a Christian Marriage*, ed. Elizabeth Fellersen (Nutley, NJ: Presbyterian and Reformed Publishing Co., 1972), 13.

ily and church as educators. The majority of parents send their children to government schools that are anti-God.

> While most Christians strongly oppose the idea that civil governments should provide cradle-to-grave security, many of them are blind on the matter of education. Somehow, we don't even question the idea of a public-school system. We don't think of ourselves as being "on welfare" when we send our kids down to the neighborhood school. We need to think about this. Socialized education is no different in principle from socialized medicine or socialized anything else. When we send the children to the government school, we are accepting tax-financed welfare.

> ———

> The public-school system is not based on charity. It is not based on the principle of voluntarism. The public schools are funded with taxes. When we enroll our children in a public school, we are stealing from our neighbors.[8]

The family serves as a dominion force, extending dominion through the establishment of additional family units (Gen. 2:24). This is why the monolithic, centralized State sees the family as a threat in its attempts to centralize power and authority.[9]

Man is responsible to God for his use of the earth, and must, as a faithful governor, discharge his calling only in terms of his

---

8. Robert Thoburn, *The Children Trap: Biblical Principles for Education* (Fort Worth and Nashville: Dominion Press/Thomas Nelson, 1986), 37.

9. The scene at the building of Babel in Genesis 11 gives us a picture of the centralization of family, church, and political entities. The many family and tribal names are merged into the "name" designated by the builders of Babel. Genesis 10 lists the many nations by their names. The building of the tower and the consolidation of the nations were in rebellion against the original dominion mandate to be "fruitful and multiply" according to families (cf. Gen. 1:26–28; 2:24).

sovereign's royal decree or word. His calling confers also on him an authority by delegation. To man is given authority by God over his household and over the earth. In the Marxist scheme, the transfer of authority from the family to the state makes any talk of the family as an institution ridiculous. The family is to all practical intent abolished whenever the state determines the education, vocation, religion, and the discipline of the child.[10]

The family is responsible for the care of its own members (1 Tim. 5:8). It's deplorable that the State has become a substitute family for many in the United States.

Maintaining the biblical family covenant is necessary for civilization to maintain itself and advance. Our nation's founders understood this principle. For example, Independence era founder James Wilson, one of only six men who signed both the Declaration of Independence and the Constitution, and who also served on the Supreme Court, wrote the following in "Of the Natural Rights of Individuals" (1790):

> Whether we consult the soundest deductions of reason, or resort to the best information conveyed to us by history, or listen to the undoubted intelligence communicated in holy writ, we shall find, that to the institution of marriage the true origin of society must be traced. By that institution the felicity of Paradise was consummated; and since the unhappy expulsion from thence, to that institution, more than to any other, has mankind been indebted for the share of peace and harmony which has been distributed among them.[11]

---

10. Rushdoony, *Institutes of Biblical Law*, 163–164.
11. *Works of the Honourable James Wilson*, 3 vols. (Clark, NJ: The Law Book Exchange,Ltd., [1804] 2005), 1:476.

John Adams, the second President of the United States, said something similar:

> The foundations of national morality must be laid in private families. In vain are schools, academies, and universities, instituted, if loose principles and licentious habits are impressed upon children in their earliest years. The mothers are the earliest and most important instructors of youth. The vices and examples of the parents cannot be concealed from the children. How is it possible that children can have any just sense of the sacred obligations of morality or religion, if, from their earliest infancy, they learn that their mothers live in habitual infidelity to their fathers, and their fathers in as constant infidelity to their mothers?[12]

The family is a child's first government and should reflect the righteous nature of God's government over us. As the family goes, so goes the nation.

---

12. John Adams, "Diary," *Works of John Adams*, 10 vols. (Boston: Little, Brown, and Company, 1865), 3:171–172.

5

Church Government Under God's Government

The church is a government ordained by God. It has rulers (overseers/elders: 1 Tim. 3:1–7), members (flock: Acts 20:28), laws (goodness of God's law: 1 Tim. 1:5–11), sanctions ("removed from your midst": 1 Cor. 5:2), and a legacy ("the gates of Hades will not overpower it": Matt. 16:18). When a dispute arises among Christians, Jesus said, "tell the church":

> If your brother sins against you, go and rebuke him in private. If he listens to you, you have won your brother. But if he won't listen, take one or two others with you, so that by the testimony of two or three witnesses every fact may be established. If he doesn't pay attention to them, **tell the church**. If he doesn't pay attention even to the church, let him be like a Gentile and a tax collector to you. Truly I tell you, whatever you bind on earth will have been bound in heaven, and whatever you loose on earth will have been loosed in heaven (Matt. 18:15–18).

For too many Christians as well as politicians, the Church is viewed more as a voluntary association than a government. In biblical terms, however, the church is a government. When the phrase "separation of church and state" was used by John Calvin, Martin Luther, and other pre-constitutional theorists, it had the meaning of *governmental* or jurisdictional separation.[1]

Like the family, the church is a divinely ordained institution. The State does not create the church and therefore cannot define it. The church is not a New Testament creation, contrary to what some theologians claim. The New Testament *ekklēsia* is an extension of the Old Testament *ekklēsia* (Acts 5:11). We learn from Acts 7:38 that the "church" (*ekklēsia*) was "in the wilderness." The first church (*ekklēsia*) was in Jerusalem (8:1–3) and consisted mostly of Jews. The more accurate translation of *ekklēsia* is "congregation" or "assembly."

The Old Testament church is not theologically distinct from the New Testament church when it comes to jurisdictional operation and separation.

1. SOVEREIGNTY: WHO'S IN CHARGE?

Ultimately, Jesus is the "head of the Church" (Eph. 5:23). God established elders to be governors in the church, not the people generally, although the people do elect officers based on experience, reputation, and evidence of good government in other areas of life (1 Cor. 3).

The authority and power given to churches (plural), in the Protestant model, is delegated, limited, and decentralized. The

---

1. Daniel L. Dreisbach, *Thomas Jefferson and the Wall of Separation Between Church and State* (New York: New York University Press, 2002), 62–67.

Bible stresses local church government. Paul's letters indicate that there were many churches in Asia Minor, Macedonia, Achaia: Colossae, Ephesus, Philippi, Thessalonica, Corinth, and Galatia. John lists seven churches, six of which are not mentioned by Paul (Rev. 2–3). There was also a church in Antioch, Jerusalem, and Rome.

Those who govern in the church are to meet certain moral standards (1 Tim. 3:1–7), like the qualifications for earthly civil rulers found under the Old Covenant (Ex. 18):

> It is a trustworthy statement: if any man aspires to the office of overseer, it is a fine work he desires to do. An overseer, then, must be above reproach, the husband of one wife, temperate, prudent, respectable, hospitable, able to teach, not addicted to wine or pugnacious, but gentle, peaceable, free from the love of money [**self-government**]. He must be one who manages his own household well, keeping his children under control with all dignity (but if a man does not know how to manage his own household, how will he take care of the church of God?) [**family government**], and not a new convert, so that he will not become conceited and fall into the condemnation incurred by the devil. And he must have a good reputation with those outside the church, so that he will not fall into reproach and the snare of the devil.

Notice how self-government and family government are indicators of what qualifies a person for church leadership. The family is the training ground for good government. It's a microcosm of what a civil or business leader will most likely do when put in positions of authority when governing other people.

2. HIERARCHY: TO WHOM
DO I REPORT?

Church government is neither a democracy nor a monarchy. There is a chain of command in church government. Leaders in the first-century church met to discuss theological issues as they arose in what has been described as "The Council at Jerusalem" (Acts 15).

As in all God-ordained governments, those in leadership positions are to be obeyed: "Obey your leaders and submit to them; for they keep watch over your souls, as those who will give an account" (Heb. 13:17a). As with self-government and family governments, ruling is not done autonomously. Church governors are not a law unto themselves. They must be held to account by the specifics of God's Word in terms of self-government, family government, and ecclesiastical government. When Paul and Silas spoke to Jews living in Berea, the Bereans "received the word with great eagerness, examining the Scriptures daily, to see whether these things were so" (Acts 17:11). Church leaders are not autonomous. They are bound by the Word of God.

There are limits to the authority of church governors as there are with all governors. They are not to lord it over the people (2 Cor. 1:24; 4:5; 11:20):

> Therefore, I exhort the elders among you, as *your* fellow elder and witness of the sufferings of Christ, and a partaker also of the glory that is to be revealed, shepherd the flock of God among you, exercising oversight not under compulsion, but voluntarily, according to the will of God; and not for sordid gain, but with eagerness; nor yet as lording it over those allotted to your charge, but proving to be examples to the flock (1 Pet. 5:3).

Peter was echoing the words of Jesus:

> But Jesus called them to Himself and said, "You know that the rulers of the Gentiles lord it over them, and their great men exercise authority over them. It is not this way among you, but whoever wishes to become great among you shall be your servant, and whoever wishes to be first among you shall be your slave; just as the Son of Man did not come to be served, but to serve, and to give His life a ransom for many" (Matt. 20:25).

Jesus is the model for church government. Servanthood-governance is the goal.

Church governors are to be appreciated and supported for their leadership role (1 Thess. 5:12) but are never to lord it over its members.

3. LAW: WHAT ARE THE RULES?

Ecclesiastical officers have jurisdictional (*juris*="law" + *diction*= "speak": to speak the law) authority to address God's law to the body of Christian believers. Christianity is not lawless: "Do we then nullify the Law through faith? May it never be! On the contrary, we establish the Law" (Rom. 3:31).

Certain parts of the Law have been changed because of a change in covenants, but the moral portion of the law remains. There are certain ecclesiastical laws that are unique to church government over which family and civil governments have no jurisdiction. This is especially true when it comes to church discipline.

Church government does not exist in isolation. The church is a servant to the world. This is why Jesus tells us to "make friends with [an] opponent at law while [he] is with him on the way, in order that [his] opponent may not deliver [him] to the judge, and the judge to the officer, and [he] be thrown into prison" (Matt. 5:25). Being at peace with the world means to be morally principled.

Paul writes that "the law is good, if it is used lawfully" (1 Tim. 1:8). He then lists some of the moral failings that can bedevil the church:

> realizing the fact that law is not made for a righteous person, but for those who are lawless and rebellious, for the ungodly and sinners, for the unholy and profane, for those who kill their fathers or mothers, for murderers and immoral men and homosexuals and kidnappers and liars and perjurers, and whatever else is contrary to sound teaching, according to the glorious gospel of the blessed God, with which I have been entrusted (vv. 9–11).

Notice that the gospel does not nullify the requirement to keep God's commandments. "For this is the love of God, **that we keep His commandments**; and His commandments are not burdensome" (1 John 5:3; also, 2:3; John 14:15; 15:10; 1 John 3:22, 24; Rev. 12:17; 14:12).

Paul tells the church leaders of Corinth to deal with a member who had committed an immoral act, an "immorality of such a kind as does not exist even among the Gentiles, that someone has his father's wife" (1 Cor. 5:1; Lev. 18:8; Deut. 22:30; 27:20). He even offers instructions on how to deal with someone who stole (Eph. 4:28) and someone who refuses to work (1 Thess. 4:11; 2 Thess. 3:10).

4. SANCTIONS: WHAT HAPPENS
IF I KEEP OR BREAK THE RULES?

There are ecclesiastical governmental sanctions that can include excommunication (Matt. 18:15–20). This is not the prerogative of a civil government.

> It is not insignificant that the Scriptures suggest that his first step should be in private [the importance of self-government and its relationship to other governments]. Before others are brought into the conflict, before witnesses or the church are included, the parties should seek a reconciliation on a personal and private basis. In such initial meetings, friends or advisors may, in fact, impede reconciliation. Others who wish to rush in quickly might note the counsel of Proverbs 26:17: "He who meddles in a quarrel not his own is like one who takes a passing dog by the ears" (RSV).[2]

There is a spiritual dimension to ecclesiastical government not found either in the family or the State (1 Cor. 5:1–8). While the family has the power of the rod, and the State has the power of the sword, the church has the power of the keys (Matt. 16:13–20).

Church governments can operate courts distinct from civil governments. While Paul discouraged lawsuits between believers, he did establish the principle that the people of God should be capable of handling disputes among the brethren: "Does any one of you, when he has a case against his neighbor, dare to go to law before the unrighteous, and not before the saints?" (1 Cor. 6:1).

---

2. Lynn R. Buzzard and Laurence Eck, *Tell it to the Church: Reconciling Out of Court* (Elgin, IL: David C. Cook, 1982), 31.

When disputes cannot be settled between two individuals or among family members, the church can (must) operate as a legitimate judicial authority to adjudicate cases where self-government has broken down.

While church governors do not have the power of the sword, they do have the power of the keys in terms of church discipline. Ecclesiastical confrontation and even excommunication used to be serious business. Consider the 1964 film *Beckett* that starred Richard Burton as Thomas Becket and Peter O'Toole as King Henry II.

Henry was in continuous conflict with the elderly Archbishop of Canterbury, who opposed the taxation of Church property that the king wanted to use to support his military campaigns in France. "Bishop, I must hire the Swiss Guards to fight for me—and no one has ever paid them off with good wishes and prayer!"

When Henry heard of the Bishop's death, he appointed his carousing friend Thomas Becket to be the new Archbishop of Canterbury. Beckett took his new ecclesiastical position seriously. He acted as an archbishop should.

Shortly thereafter, Becket sided with the Church, throwing Henry into a protesting fury. One of the main bones of contention is Thomas' excommunication of Lord Gilbert, one of Henry's most loyal supporters, for seizing and ordering the killing of a priest who had been accused of sexual indiscretions with a young girl, before the priest could be handed over for an ecclesiastical trial. Gilbert then refused to acknowledge his transgressions and seek absolution.

The battle between king and bishop continued until Beckett was murdered and Henry finally repented.

Today, what should the Roman Catholic Church leadership do when its members vote to permit the killing of babies in the womb and support same-sex marriage? New York Governor Andrew Cuomo denounced the teachings of his own church and dismissed its ecclesiastical authority. The church was obligated to discipline the governor and any other politician supporting the killing of unborn babies. While the church canot remove him from his political office, it can excommunicate him from church and treat him as an unbeliever.

5. LEGACY: DOES CHURCH GOVERNMENT HAVE A FUTURE?

The church is told to avoid Israel's mistakes, or it will suffer the same fate (1 Cor. 10:1–15). God issued a similar warnings to the churches of Asia Minor (Rev. 2–3).

In the former Soviet Union, for example, Christians were forbidden to "set up benefit societies, cooperatives of industrial societies; to offer material aid to [their] members; to organize children's and young persons' groups for prayer and other purposes, or general biblical, literary or handicraft groups for the purpose of work or religious instruction and the like, or to organize groups, circles, or sections; to arrange excursions and kindergartens, open libraries and reading rooms, organize sanatoria or medical aid."[3]

Prior to these oppressive conditions, the church could have done something and did not. One might even be able to make

---

3. "Concerning religious societies," Resolution of the Central Committee, 8 April 1929, para. 17. Cited in Evgeny Barabanov, "The Schism Between the Church and the World," *From Under the Rubble*, ed. Alexander Solzhenitsyn (Boston, MA: Little, Brown and Company, 1975), 180.

the case that the Russian church's *lack* of social involvement had a part to play in the 1917 revolution that led to religious and political oppression and the spread of Communism around the world.

Here's just one example: "It is a sad but irrefutable fact that the Russian Orthodox Church at the time of the Bolshevik Revolution was engaged in a fruitless attempt to preserve its religious treasures (chalices, vestments, paintings, icons, etc.) and was therefore unable to relate meaningfully to the tremendous social upheavals then taking place."[4]

Once the old corrupt government fell and the repressive regime of the Marxists came to power, strategies for reform had to be rethought. In a nation under repressive domination, the most immediate need of the Christian community is the production of Christian literature, family instruction, worship, prayer, and ways to keep their efforts secret, not grand efforts of social reform that have no chance of success. The goal is to wait out the inevitable collapse of the illegitimate political system and be ready to replace it when it falls (2 Tim. 3:7–9).

Once the iron curtain fell, it was learned that Christians were at the forefront of many of the efforts to topple communism and bring about reform from the inside. When they had an opportunity to institute change, Christians took advantage of the window of opportunity in a big way. Rev. Laszlo Tokes, the Hungarian pastor who sparked the Romanian revolution, stated that Eastern Europe is not just in a political revolution but a religious renaissance. Instead of being executed, Rev. Tokes believed he was saved through "divine intervention."

---

4. Donald G. Bloesch, *Crumbling Foundations: Death and Rebirth in an Age of Upheaval* (Grand Rapids, MI: Zondervan, 1984), 30.

"The reports that reached the western news media recounted references to Jesus, the Christian spirit, and Czechoslovakia's role as the 'spiritual crossroads of Europe.'"[5] It was not enough for these Christians to be free to worship. They also wanted to participate in every facet of their nation's life. The church in Czechoslovakia did not take a "hands off" approach to social issues once the iron curtain began to crumble. The Christian leadership saw it as their duty to bring effectual change to the broader culture.

Josef Tson followed a similar path in Romania as early as 1947. Tson told a friend that "Communism is an experiment that has failed. It wasn't able to fulfill any of its promises and nobody believes in it anymore. Because of this, it will one day collapse on its own.... When communism collapses, somebody has to be there to rebuild society! I believe our job as Christian teachers is to train leaders so that they will be ready and capable to rebuild our society on a Christian basis."[6]

Tson started a training program in 1981 for Christian leaders who remained in Romania. The Communist regime eventually fell, and Nicolae Ceausescu and his wife were captured and executed on December 25, 1989. Tson had trained more than a thousand people all over Romania. Today, these people are the leaders in churches, evangelical denominations, and key Christian ministries.

Reform efforts can never stop. Christians must be eternally vigilant. On July 1, 2003, Tokes warned the young people of

---

5. Barbara Reynolds, "Religion is greatest story ever missed," *USA Today* (March 16, 1990), 13A.

6. Josef Tson, "The Cornerstone at the Crossroads," *Wheaton Alumni* (August/September 1991).

Romania that "'foreign' values and mentalities, such as communism, materialism, imperialism and internationalism, imposed on us before 1989, are surviving in Romania, dressed up in a 'Social Democratic coat.'" His message was the same: "We need to return to the Christian civic system of values."[7]

Barbara Ehrenreich, author of a number of books pushing Marxist ideology and articles hostile to the role of Christianity and politics, claims that the "fear of governmental tyranny kept the Founding Fathers from prescribing anything like 'family values.' Homosexuality was not unknown 200 years ago; nor was abortion. But these were matters, like religion, that the founders left to individual conscience."[8]

This is a remarkable assertion since the thirteen colonies that became our nation's first thirteen states had laws on the books making sodomy a crime. In some cases, sodomy was punished by death![9] In *Bowers vs. Hardwick* (1986) the court remarked in some detail:

> Sodomy was a criminal offense at common law and was forbidden by the laws of the original 13 States when they ratified the Bill of Rights. In 1868, when the Fourteenth Amendment was ratified, all but 5 of the 37 States in the Union had criminal sodomy laws. In fact, until 1961, all 50 States outlawed sodomy, and today [1986], 25 States and the District of Columbia

---

7. Nora Georgescu, "UDMR [Democratic Hungarian Union of Romania] radicals raise a profile again" (July 1, 2003).

8. Barbara Ehrenreich, "Why the Religious Right Is Wrong," *Time* (September 7, 1992), 72.

9. "Trials for sex crimes [in early Massachusetts] were occasionally noted but there was only one recorded execution." Edwin Powers, *Crime and Punishment in Early Massachusetts, 1620–1692: A Documentary History* (Boston, MA: Beacon Press, 1966), 300.

continue to provide criminal penalties for sodomy performed in private and between consenting adults.[10]

Sodomy has never been tolerated in our nation's history. The law codes of fifty states prove it.

At a general court-martial, on March 10, 1778, a Lieutenant Enslin was "tried for attempting to commit sodomy with John Monhort." He was also tried for "Perjury in swearing to false Accounts." Enslin was "found guilty of the charges exhibited against him, being breaches of 5th. Article 18th. Section of the Articles of War." He was dismissed from the service "with infamy. His Excellency the Commander in Chief [George Washington] approve[d] the sentence and with Abhorrence and Detestation of such infamous Crimes order[ed] Lieutt. Enslin to be drummed out of the Camp... by all the Drummers and Fifers in the Army never to return."[11]

Ehrenreich also wants us to believe that there were no laws prohibiting abortion until the Christian Right came along. This is nonsense. She needs to be reminded that abortion was legalized in 1973—nearly two hundred years after the ratification of the Constitution. Prior to the *Roe vs. Wade* decision, abortion was outlawed in all fifty states and the District of Columbia, with exceptions only for life endangerment of the mother.[12] Isn't

10. *Bowers vs. Hardwick*, 478 US 186, 92 L Ed 2d 140, 106 S Ct 2841, reh den (US) 92 L Ed 2d 779, 107 S. Ct 29., 14748. The plaintiff in the Hardwick case was caught engaging in the act of sodomy only after the police entered the house on an unrelated case.

11. *The Writings of George Washington, Bicentennial Edition*, 39 vols. (Washington, DC: U.S. Government Printing Office, 1934), (March 1 through May 31, 1778), 11:83–84.

12. David Granfield, *The Abortion Decision* (Garden City, NY: Doubleday, 1969), 78–80. Ehrenreich signed, along with more than 400 other pro-abortionists, an *amicus curia* brief in the 1989 *Webster v. Reproductive Health Ser-*

this a perfect example of the "family values" which Ehrenreich tells us were not legislated?

Ehrenreich and her liberal peers are determined to ignore the historical record and to remake the founders in their own image. Both Jefferson and Washington believed that without religion, America's civil life would be chaotic. The legal decisions and public pronouncements of this nation attest to this fact: the "family values" that the liberal left disdains are rooted deeply in our heritage and are based on nothing other than principles of God's Word.

---

vices. The purpose of the brief was to demonstrate historically that "Through the nineteenth century American common-law decisions uniformly reaffirmed that women committed no offense in seeking abortions." The assertion is false. See Ramesh Ponnuru, "Aborting History," *National Review* (October 23, 1995), 29–32. Also see Marvin Olasky, *Abortion Rites: A Social History of Abortion in America* (Wheaton, IL: Crossway Books, 1992).

6

Civil Government Under God's Government

Moses faced a problem. Everyone seemed to be suing everyone else, and they had only been out of Egypt for a month. Slaves often cannot govern themselves well because their ability to govern independent of an authoritative master was denied them. Self-government and family government are dangerous to slaveholders. These recent slaves could not settle their own disputes. So, they lined up in front of Moses' tent daily to have him settle their quarrels. Jethro, Moses' father-in-law, saw what was happening. He suggested a fundamental set of principles to governing well (Ex. 18:17–27).

First, Moses was to serve as God's representative, an intermediary between Him and the people. Of course, this situation was unique to Israel, but the principle of earthly governmental representatives remains. Second, teach the people God's law so they can learn to govern themselves. Third, establish an appeals court system, with righteous and experienced men serving as judges. Let these governors take the easier cases, saving the difficult cases for Moses to take before God.

What was the more fundamental principle Jethro was trying to convey to Moses and us?

> You are not God. Acknowledge your weaknesses and limitations. Share in the authority of being a judge, and you will not wear out these people and they will not wear you out. In short, don't imitate the Pharaohs who thought of themselves as gods whose word was the word of the gods because they saw themselves as an extension of deity. Don't treat the people as slaves, even if they want to be slaves. Slavery is the way of destruction. God has delivered you out of Egypt. Do not go back to Egypt governmentally.

Jethro recognized a basic fact of institutional life: the second point in the biblical covenant—the necessity of hierarchy and delegated authority under God. There must be a system of policymaking and a process for appeals. To what extent are policies set at the top and at the bottom? Where does primary institutional sovereignty lie, at the top or the bottom? The question facing Moses was this: Which kind of human hierarchical authority structure is required by God, top-down or bottom-up?

God has established a bottom-up system of multiple hierarchies: family, church, and State (civil governments). This means that we must always be obedient *where obedience is required by God's law*. The appeals court system of Exodus 18:17–27 is a good guide: we are free only when we obey God, and we must subject our actions to scrutiny by lawful, God-ordained, covenantal authorities in church, family, and the civil sphere. The Bible directs us to submit to every human institution but with certain *limitations.* "Whether to a king as the one in authority, or to governors as sent by him for the punishment of evildoers and the praise of those who do right" (1 Peter 2:13). While Peter has civil authority in mind here, this text is inclusive enough to include family and church authorities. As Bible-believing Christians we must always remember that when we speak of authority, we mean more than *civil* authority. In addition, we must recognize and insist that these governors are bound by God's commandments in their jurisdictional duties. As we are required to submit, they also are bound to submit to God's law.

The apostle Paul goes so far as to put ecclesiastical authority on an equal par with the civil courts: "Does any one of you, when he has a case against his neighbor, dare to go to law before the unrighteous, and not before the saints? Or do you not know that the saints will judge the world? And if the world is judged by you, are you not competent to constitute the smallest law courts?" (1 Cor. 6:1–11). The civil sphere does not have exclusive jurisdictional authority.

As citizens of political jurisdictions, Christians must submit themselves to those who rule because God has established the civil realm by His own sovereign will (Rom. 13:1). Keep in mind, however, that civil authorities are not absolute in the way they exercise their authority since they are bound by what's good and evil. Governors do not have the right or authority to define what's good and evil.

Rulers should not be cursed by the people: "You shall not curse God, nor curse a ruler of your people" (Ex. 22:28; cf. Rom. 13:1). This does not mean, however, that the sinful practices and policies of rulers either represent God or should go unnoticed and therefore unchallenged (cf. Mark 6:18). Moreover, Christian citizens are under obligation to disobey those laws that prohibit worship and the proclamation of the gospel (Dan. 3; Acts 4:18; 5:29). In addition, a law that forces people to assent to immoral acts must also be disobeyed (Ex. 1:15–22). Jesus made it clear that evil rulers must be exposed publicly as evil rulers (cf. Luke 13:32).

OLD TESTAMENT EXAMPLES

The Hebrew midwives were commanded by "the king of Egypt" to put to death all the male children being born to the Hebrew women (Ex. 1:15–16). The Hebrew midwives disobeyed the edict of the king: "But the midwives feared God and did not do as the king of Egypt had commanded them, but let the boys live" (1:17). God shows He approved of their actions: "So God was good to the midwives, and the people multiplied, and became very mighty. And it came about because the midwives feared God, that He established households for them" (1:20–21).

Jochebed, Moses' mother, also disobeyed the edict of the king by hiding her child and later creating a way of escape so he would not be murdered by the king's army: "But when she could hide him no longer, she got him a wicker basket and covered it over with tar and pitch. Then she put the child into it and set it among the reeds by the bank of the Nile" (2:3). Jochebed even deceived Pharaoh's daughter into believing that she was in no way related to the child (2:7–9).

Rahab hid the spies of Israel and lied about their whereabouts. When a route for escape became available, she led them out another way from that of the pursuing soldiers. She is praised by two New Testament writers for her actions: "By faith Rahab the harlot did not perish along with those who were disobedient, after she had welcomed the spies in peace" (Heb. 11:31). Rahab is listed with Abraham as one whose faith was reflected in her works: "And in the same way [as Abraham] was not Rahab the harlot also justified by works, when she received the messengers and sent them out by another way?" (James 2:25). By sending the spies out by another way, she subverted the king's objective to capture the spies.

Shadrach, Meshach, and Abednego refused to follow the command of the king to worship the golden statue: "These men, king, have disregarded you; they do not serve your gods or worship the golden image you have set up" (Dan. 3:12). When the three were thrown into the furnace, the angel of the Lord came to their aid (3:25).

King Darius signed a document that prohibited anyone from making "a petition to any god or man besides" himself (Dan. 6:7). Anyone refusing to obey the order "shall be cast into the lion's den." Daniel refused to obey. The Bible states that Daniel went out of his way to disobey the order: "Now when Daniel knew that the document was signed, he entered his house (now in his roof chamber he had windows open toward Jerusalem); and he continued kneeling on his knees three times a day, praying and giving thanks before his God, as he had been doing previously" (6:10).

David, while honoring King Saul as God's anointed, escaped from him and did not submit to his vengeful authority. He even picked up Goliath's sword for protection (1 Sam. 21:9). Saul showed himself to be a tyrant by demanding that the priests at Nob be killed (22:11–23). The guards rebelled and refused. Saul then turned to Doeg the Edomite to do the dirty deed.

"He attacked the priests, and he killed that day eighty-five men who wore the linen ephod" (22:18). David was a fugitive for a just cause, and God protected him from Saul (23:14).

NEW TESTAMENT EXAMPLES

The New Testament has similar accounts of resistance to tyranny. When Peter and John were ordered by the rulers and elders of the people to stop preaching in the name of Jesus (Acts 4:18), the two apostles refused to follow the prohibition: "Whether it is right in the sight of God to give heed to you rather than to God, you be the judge; for we cannot stop speaking what we have seen and heard" (4:19–20). Peter and John could not stop speaking what they had seen and heard because they had been commanded by Jesus to preach in His name (cf. Matt. 28:18–20; Acts 1:8; 1 Cor. 9:16).

On another occasion, some of the apostles were arrested for preaching and healing in the name of Jesus. Again, they were put in a "public jail" (Acts 5:18). During the night "an angel of the Lord...opened the gates of the prison" and commanded them to disobey the rulers of Israel: "Go your way, stand and speak to the people in the temple the whole message of life" (5:20). When the apostles again were confronted with the command not to preach and teach, their response was quick and sure: "We must obey God rather than men" (5:29).

The apostles' obedience to God conflicted with the laws of the existing authorities. This resulted in the first apostolic death: "Now about that time Herod the king [Agrippa I] laid hands on some who belonged to the church, to mistreat them. And he had James the brother of John put to death" (Acts 12:1–2). Peter was later arrested for similar "crimes" against the State (12:3). There is no indication that God showed His disapproval of their rebellion against the actions of these authorities in these specific cases. He even sent one of His angels to release Peter from prison (12:6–8). There are several such cases where divine assistance released outspoken Christians from the hands of the State.

When Paul and Silas were arrested and had "many blows inflicted upon them" (Acts 16:23) it did not end there. The jailer reported the following to Paul, saying, "The chief magistrates have sent to release you. Therefore, come out now and go in peace." But Paul said to them, "They have beaten us in public without trial, men who are Romans, and have thrown us into prison; and now are they sending us away secretly? No indeed! But let them come themselves and bring us out."

> The policemen reported these words to the chief magistrates. They were afraid when they heard that they were Romans, and they came and appealed to them, and when they had brought them out, they kept begging them to leave the city. They went out of the prison and entered the house of Lydia, and when they saw the brethren, they encouraged them and departed (16:36–40).

These examples show that while Peter's instructions regarding "every human institution" (1 Peter 2:13), seems absolute. It's obvious that when all of God's revelation is taken into account there are exceptions.

Thus, there can be no question of the legality of resistance to evil earthly authorities. The best approach is for another lawful authority, such as parents, local church elders or a denomination, local church, state rulers (governor and legislature) or county officials to intercede. This is a now unfamiliar doctrine of the Protestant Reformation called "the doctrine of interposition." John Calvin explains it in his *Institutes of the Christian Religion*.[1] It also was one of the legal justifications for the War for Independence[2] where duly constituted state governments pushed back against another governing authority.

A REAL LIFE EXAMPLE

Christianity was considered a threat to the governing authorities in Nazi Germany, similar to what's now taking place in China, Islamic nations, and in parts of the United States. Over time, churches were "confined as far as possible to the performance of narrowly religious functions, and even within this narrow sphere were subjected to as many hindrances as the Nazis dared to impose."

This is the evaluation of a 1945 report published by the Office of Strategic Services (OSS), the precursor to the CIA. It was called *The Nazi Master Plan: The Persecution of the Christian Churches* and was prepared for the War Crimes Staff. It offered the following summary: "This study describes, with illustrative factual evidence, Nazi purposes, policies and methods of persecuting the Christian Churches in Germany and occupied Europe."

Where did the strategic plan begin? "Implementation of this objective started with the curtailment of religious instruction in the primary and secondary schools with the squeezing of the

---

1. Michael Gilstrap, "John Calvin's Theology of Resistance," in Gary North, ed., *The Theology of Christian Resistance*, Christianity and Civilization 2, Symposium on (1983), 180–217.

2. Tom Rose, "On Reconstruction and the American Republic," *Theology of Christian Resistance, Christianity and Civilization* 2, 285–310.

religious periods into inconvenient hours, with Nazi propagandists among the teachers in order to induce them to refuse the teaching of religion, with vetoing of . . . religious textbooks, and finally with substituting [a] Nazi *Weltanschauung* [worldview] and 'German faith' for Christian religious denominational instruction. . . . At the time of the outbreak of the war . . . religious instruction had practically disappeared from Germany's primary schools."

The next step was to neutralize the impact that churches would have on politics. "Under the pretext that the Churches themselves were interfering in political and state matters, [the Nazis] would deprive the Churches, step by step, of all opportunity to affect German public life."[3] How often do we hear that the "separation between church and state" means that churches must remain silent on social and political issues and that pastors cannot use their pulpits (unless they're liberal) to influence legislation?

When Martin Niemoeller used his pulpit to expose Adolf Hitler's radical politics, "He knew every word spoken was reported by Nazi spies and secret agents."[4] Leo Stein describes in his book *I Was in Hell with Niemoeller* how the Gestapo gathered evidence against Niemoeller:

> Now, the charge against Niemoeller was based entirely on his sermons, which the Gestapo agents had taken down stenographically. But in none of his sermons did Pastor Niemoeller exhort his congregation to overthrow the Nazi regime. He merely

---

3. *The Nazi Master Plan: The Persecution of the Christian Churches: Annex 4: The Persecution of the Christian Churches* (July 6, 1945): https://bit.ly/3iZZ1Nk

4. Basil Miller, *Martin Niemoeller: Hero of the Concentration Camp*, 5th ed. (Grand Rapids, MI: Zondervan, 1942), 112.

raised his voice against some of the Nazi policies, particularly the policy directed against the Church. He had even refrained from criticizing the Nazi government itself or any of its personnel. Under the former government his sermons would have been construed only as an exercise of the right of free speech. Now, however, written laws, no matter how explicitly they were worded, were subjected to the interpretation of the judges.[5]

In a June 27, 1937 sermon, Niemoeller made it clear to those in attendance that they had a sacred duty to speak out on the evils of the Nazi regime no matter what the consequences:

> We have no more thought of using our own powers to escape the arm of the authorities than had the Apostles of old. No more are we ready to keep silent at man's behest when God commands us to speak. For it is, and must remain, the case that we must obey God rather than man.[6]

A few days later, Niemoeller was arrested. His crime? "Abuse of the pulpit." The "Special Courts" set up by the Nazis made claims against pastors who spoke out against Hitler's policies. Niemoeller was not the only one singled out by the Gestapo. "Some 807 other pastors and leading laymen of the 'Confessional Church' were arrested in 1937, and hundreds more in the next couple of years."[7]

A group of Confessional Churches in Germany, founded by Pastor Niemoeller and other Protestant ministers, drew up

---

5. Leo Stein, *I Was in Hell with Niemoeller* (New York: Fleming H. Revell, 1942), 175.

6. Quoted in William L. Shirer, *The Rise and Fall of the Third Reich* (New York: Simon and Schuster, 1960), 239.

7. Shirer, *The Rise and Fall of the Third Reich*, 239.

a proclamation to confront the political changes taking place in Germany that threatened the people "with a deadly danger. The danger lies in a new religion," the proclamation declared. "The church has by order of its Master to see to it that in our people Christ is given the honor that is proper to the Judge of the world.... The First Commandment says 'Thou shalt have no other gods before me.' The new religion is a rejection of the First Commandment."[8]

PRAYING FOR CIVIL SERVANTS

Our rulers need the prayers of Christians. First, to give them support for the difficult tasks that surely burden them. The work of the civil magistrate is multifaceted. There are constant pressures that weigh heavily on the office of each civil representative. A minister in the civil sphere must keep his own house in order as well as the house of State. Family responsibilities are often neglected for the supposed urgency of civil affairs. There is the constant barrage of special interest groups wanting to turn the civil sphere of government into a vehicle to engineer society through power and coercion. The temptation to appease these groups is great.

Second, to have God change their minds when they stray from the principles of Scripture. I can remember talking with a congressman about the abortion issue. He told me that he would not change his mind no matter what argument he heard. This is certainly presumption and arrogance. The Christian is as-

8. Quoted in Eugene Davidson, *The Trials of the Germans: An Account of the Twenty-Two Defendants before the International Military Tribunal at Nuremberg* (Columbia, MO: University of Missouri Press, [1966] 1997), 275.

sured that God is in control of the king's heart: "The king's heart is like channels of water in the hand of the LORD; He turns it wherever He wishes" (Prov. 21:1). There is a biblical precedence for this attitude. Pharaoh would not listen to the arguments of Moses. God made Pharaoh a believer, the hard way (Ex. 3–15).

Third, to give them wisdom in applying the absolutes of God's Word to civil situations. This was Solomon's prayer (1 Kings 3). There was no specific law that Solomon referenced in the way he handled the case of the two women who claimed a baby was theirs (1 Kings 3:16–28). The Bible calls on us to "search the Scriptures daily" (Acts 17:11) so our senses will be trained to discern good and evil (Heb. 5:14).

Fourth, to pray for a well-ordered State so the church of Jesus Christ is protected and given freedom in preaching the gospel. The State must protect the Christian religion. Any obstacle that would jeopardize the preaching of the Word of God in carrying out the Great Commission must be removed by civil government. The apostle Paul instructs Christians to pray for those who rule so "that we [Christians] may lead a tranquil and quiet life in all godliness and dignity" (1 Tim. 2:2).

In another place Paul appeals to the civil magistrate for protection from those who were threatening the Christian religion and his own life as a minister of the gospel (Acts 23:12–31; cf. 25:11). This means that civil government cannot be religiously neutral. If the Christian religion is not protected and made foundational, then some other religion will be, usually a State religion that degenerates into paganism. The State must go beyond mere toleration (the acceptance of all religions as long as those religions do not conflict with the operations of the State) and maintain religious freedom for Christian churches.

INSTRUCTING CIVIL RULERS

Jesus told His early disciples that they would be "brought before governors and kings for His sake" (Matt. 10:18), and they were as the book of Acts makes clear. The apostle Paul declared, "Woe is me if I do not preach the gospel" (1 Cor. 9:16). When Paul was brought before the civil officials of Rome, he was obligated, for he was under compulsion by God, to preach the gospel. King Agrippa was confronted with the claims of Jesus Christ and responded by saying, "In a short time you will persuade me to become a Christian" (Acts 26:28). Paul responds by saying, "I pray to God that whether in a short or long time, not only you, but also all who hear me this day, might become such as I am, except for these chains" (v. 29).

It is not enough to have "conservative" rulers who implement a pragmatic approach to governing. Christians should be working for *Christian* leaders whose lives are conformed to the image of Jesus Christ and who seek to make the Word of God "in terms of its civil principles" applicational to civil government.

Civil governments have the responsibility to punish evil doers and promote the good. The task of civil governments at all levels is to exercise their limited but necessary authority in their jurisdictions and settle disputes between conflicting jurisdictions. When disputes and/or crimes are committed, the civil magistrates at all levels of governance must act swiftly and justly. The standard of judgment is the Word of God, "for it [the God-ordained authority] is a minister of God to you for good" (Rom. 13:4). Notice that Paul declares that the civil magistrate is required to be minister to you for "good." Paul has a biblical moral order in mind when he speaks about the operation of those in a civil capacity.

In the Old Testament, priests and judges who were experts in the law of God instructed the king on how he should apply the details of the law to various civil issues (Deut. 17:8–12, 18–20). Unfortunately, the church no longer sees its calling as prophetic. Of course, there are those in the civil sphere who despise the absolutes of God's Word and anyone who would hold them accountable.

PURSUING PEACE

Peace can only be realized through the life-transforming gospel of Jesus Christ. Genuine and lasting peace will not come through law, force, political promises or compromises, the elimination of poverty, the establishment of a one-world humanistic government, or the military threat of Mutual Assured Destruction (MAD). To pray for peace, as we are instructed to do, cannot be a substitute for the preaching of the gospel so that the nations are discipled according to the Word of Jesus Christ (Matt. 28:20).

Wars do not often arise because from environmental factors. Rather, they are the result of man's inherent sinfulness and desire for power, territory, and wealth: "What is the source of quarrels and conflicts among you? Is not the source your pleasures that wage war in your members? You lust and do not have; so you commit murder. And you are envious and cannot obtain; so you fight and quarrel" (James 4:1–2). If this is true of the Christian community, should we expect anything less among non-Christians? The Ninth Tenth Commandment forbids covetousness. War is a form of covetousness.

RENDERING TO CAESAR

Because civil governments are ordained by God and act as ministerial institutions (Rom. 13:4), they need financing to pay for specific rendered services. Caesar rendered a service: "Render to Caesar the things that are Caesar's; and to God the things that are God's" (Matt. 22:21). Jesus certainly was not endorsing the way Caesar governed in all cases, but He was, at least, upholding the biblical institution of civil government and its authority to limited taxation. Of course, those "things that are Caesar's" are not his by edict or whim. Rather, they fall within the parameters of God's ordination of Caesar's jurisdiction. Jesus was not giving absolute authority to Caesar as the civil representative of the State to do anything he desired to do.

But what about those who maintain that civil rulers are taking more than their God-ordained share? This is why Christian involvement in the political sphere is necessary and mandatory. If the civil government is taxing people for redistribution purposes, contrary to the Bible and the Constitution, it is the Christian's duty to reject wealth redistribution and vote for leaders (civil ministers) who will only tax for services that are specified biblical, and in the case of our "Caesar," constitutional. At every opportunity we should work to limit authority, cut taxes, and reduce expenditures.

For the Romans, lordship was personified in the Emperor. For the Jew, therefore, paying taxes was believed to be an acknowledgment of the Roman gods. This is made clear by the stamp of the emperor's face on the coin of the realm: "TI[berius] CAESAR DIVI AUG[usti] F[ilius] AUGUSTUS," or, in translation, "Tiberius Caesar Augustus, son of the deified Augustus." Oppressive taxation always indicates that the people in general have rejected God. High taxes are a judgment of God, just like military defeats, and economic crises. The only way to overthrow political oppression through taxation is to repent before God and acknowledge that He alone is Savior, Lord, and King.

But what of the faithful? They know that the State is not God. Two points should be kept in mind. First, it may be that, while many Christians do not *believe* the State is god, nevertheless they often *act* as if it is. Second, those Christians who do not believe the State is god or act as if it is are not admitting the State is god by paying a tax. Scripture tells us that "by nature" the State, or anything else, is not God (Gal. 4:8). We pay the tax "for conscience sake" (Rom. 13:5), "lest we give them offense" (Matt. 17:27). The faithful Christian works for the day when the State will stop acting as a god and the people will stop living as if the State is a god. This won't happen if Christians abandon the political sphere.

SUPPORTING RIGHTEOUS LEADERSHIP

The people have the responsibility to support righteous leadership, but sometimes there are few viable options. The process of training and appointing or voting for leaders who are guided by God's Word may take a long time. The pool of capable civil rules may be small, but in time, if Christians take an active role in every area of life, we can make transformational changes at every level of society. We must remember that at the time of Jesus' ministry, the Roman Empire dominated. In time, however, Christians changed the political landscape.

Moses chose leaders who had already come through the ranks of family, business, and community leadership: "Choose wise and discerning and experienced men from your tribes, and I will appoint them as your heads" (Deut. 1:13). The responsibility for choosing godly leaders rested with the people. Moses then chose from those presented to him as worthy leaders: "So I took the heads of your tribes, wise and experienced men, and appointed them heads over you, leaders of thousands, and of hundreds, of fifties and of tens, and officers for your tribes" (1:15). Judges were chosen with the same moral and experiential considerations (1:16–17).

In time, however, Israel rejected this procedure and chose a different standard for determining leadership. An autonomous choice was made. The people wanted a king "like all the nations," someone who would meet their desires rather than God's requirements (1 Sam. 8:5). They rejected biblical law and voted for the "Law of the Nations," a distorted law that puts the creature at the center of lawmaking. God warned them that such an allegiance would bring only tyranny, despotism, and eventual slavery (1 Sam. 8:10–48). The rejection of biblical law resulted in the State determining what would be right and wrong.

Long-term, the State is the law under such governing principles. All those who reject the king's law are either killed or enslaved (1 Kings 12:6–15). Today, Christians have the freedom and duty to vote for responsible leadership using the standard of God's law as the measuring device for their political choice: "By the blessing of the upright a city is exalted, but by the mouth of the wicked it is torn down" (Prov. 11:11). There is a direct relationship between those who rule and the condition of the nation: "When the righteous increase, the people rejoice, but when a wicked man rules, people groan" (Prov. 29:2). The people chose a "king like all the nations." God gave them what they wanted. Christians who refuse to vote, for whatever reason, are getting what their non-vote brings.

QUALIFIED TO LEAD

The qualifications for leadership are ethical and practical, that is, they are to have some leadership experience in the family, church, school, or business world. Rulers must be "men of truth, those who hate dishonest gain" (Ex. 18:21). The standard by which they are to govern is not to be their own, and no amount of monetary and political gain will move them from their allegiance to God and His Word. They are to "fear God." This is the ethical dimension.

The apostle Paul builds on these principles when he sets forth the qualifications of leadership in the church. Ethical considerations abound. Self-government must first be manifested in a potential leader. Leaders must be able to control their own appetites (1 Tim. 3:1–7); that is, they must be self-disciplined in all their affairs. Paul draws on the Old Testament system of government that applied to both church and State, and he carries these principles to the New Testament people of God.

In addition to ethical qualifications, there are practical considerations as well. The ethical leads to the practical. The individual who is scrupulous in personal, family, and business affairs will gain positions of leadership where experience is cultivated. Those who are faithful in small things (an ethical evaluation) will be entrusted with greater responsibilities (a practical result) (Matt. 25:23). This is why the young are discouraged from holding positions of authority without some supervision or accountability. New converts are susceptible to conceit because they have not gained the needed maturity to work out the implications of their new faith in Christ (1 Tim. 3:6).

Jethro's advice to Moses suggests that "able men" must rule (Ex. 18:21). Ability is cultivated through time as the Word of God is applied to various life situations. Of course, there are rare exceptions to this general rule. Timothy is told, "Let no one look down on your youthfulness..." (1 Tim. 4:12). Paul continued to serve as a mentor to Timothy. Instead, he was to conduct himself in a way that reflects his faith in ethical terms. His life (ethical behavior) is to be an example (practical behavior) for others to imitate.

> According to Acts 16:1–3, Paul met Timothy while he was traveling through Lystra. Paul discovered that Timothy was the son of a believing Jewess and a Greek father and that people spoke highly of him. A good reputation was a characteristic that Paul valued immensely [1 Tim 3:7]. In fact, after revealing Timothy's excellent reputation, Acts 16:3 clearly states that "Paul wanted to take him along on the journey." It was at this moment that the loving mentor relationship between Paul and Timothy began.[9]

Civil leadership, like ecclesiastical leadership, is designed to be ministerial. Those in authority must follow the pattern of God as *ministers* rather than attempt to define the role of gov-

---

9. Stact E. Hoehl, "The Mentor Relationship: An Exploration of Paul as Loving Mentor to Timothy and the Application of this Relationship to Contemporary Leadership Challenges," *Journal of Biblical Perspectives in Leadership*, 3:2 (Summer 2011), 32–47.

ernmental leadership in terms of how others rule (Luke 22:24–30; cf. 1 Sam. 8:5).

Civil government is not a "necessary evil." God established the civil sphere of government like He established the family and church—for our good. What is missing in each of these governments is leadership based on an external and eternal standard of righteousness. We're often faced with voting for the best of two bad choices. It's hard to find men of principle, men who "fear God rather than man." This either/or voting option will only be remedied when the people are informed on the biblical model for governments and vote accordingly.

But where is leadership cultivated? The family and church and the educational systems they create (including internships) are the training grounds for developing true civil servants. The example of Christ as the servant par excellence is our model. Most governmental leaders are persuaded by their voting constituency. If the people back home want some law passed that will favor their district or them personally, their congressman will seek out their wishes and vote accordingly. Politicians are slaves to the will of the people. Their impetus for action is not principle but pressure. This is not the biblical model.

Civil rulers must hear from the Christian citizenry so that they uphold their oath and vote accordingly. Christians are inheritors of the earth because we are "fellow-heirs with Christ" (Rom. 8:17). We have a stake in the way our world is being run.

7

Jurisdictional Separation Under God's Government

Decentralizing the authority and power of governments has a long history, going back to the Old Testament. Moses became the chief judicial officer in Israel, assisted by numerous lesser *civil* magistrates (Ex. 18:17–26). Aaron, Moses' brother, became the chief *ecclesiastical* officer as High Priest, assisted by numerous lesser priests (29:1–9; Lev. 8). Moses did not carry out the duties of a priest, and Aaron did not perform civil tasks.

In the days of the Judges, Othniel, Ehud, Shamgar, Gideon, and Samson served as civil officers (Judges 1–13), while Phineas, Eli, and the Levites served in an ecclesiastical capacity (Judges 17; 20:28; 1 Sam. 1–8).

During the period of the monarchy, King Saul served as a civil official while Ahimelech ministered as the chief ecclesiastical leader in the nation (1 Sam. 10 and 21). David was king while Abiathar carried out the duties of a priest (1 Chron. 15:11). David's son Solomon ruled as a civil officer while Zadok pursued ecclesiastical obligations (1 Kings 1:45). King Joash and Jehoiada the priest (2 Kings 11) and King Josiah and the priest Hilkiah (2 Kings 22:4) maintained jurisdictional separation. Even after the return from exile, Church and State as parallel and jurisdictionally separate institutions operated with Governor Nehemiah (Neh. 7) and Priest Ezra (Neh. 8).

JURISDICTIONAL COOPERATION

In biblical terms, there was never such a jurisdictional separation between Church and State that the State was free from God's law (Deut. 17:15–20). Both priest and king were required to sit before the law to be instructed. The priest was to follow guidelines pertaining to ecclesiastical affairs, while the king would glean from Scripture those directives designed for his civil office. If a case was too difficult for the civil ruler to decide, the Bible gives the following instruction: "You shall come to the Levitical priest or the judge who is in office in those days, and you shall inquire of them, and they will declare to you the verdict in the case" (17:9).

Notice the use of "the Levitical priest or the judge." Both were required to be experts in the law. The judges did not follow a different standard in adjudicating legal issues. The Levites were to assist the civil ruler as much as the judges, but the Levites were not called on to rule in place of the king.

King David did not dismiss the exhortation of the prophet Nathan after being confronted for his sins of adultery and murder. Although David at first did not know that the rebuke was leveled against him, he did not act as if it was unusual for someone in Nathan's position to seek the counsel of the king and even to offer the king advice. David accepted Nathan's rebuke. He did not tell Nathan that there is a "separation between Church and State": "Then David said to Nathan, 'I have sinned against the LORD'" (2 Sam. 12:13). Modern-day separationists are closer to the way Herod responded when John the Baptist rebuked him for his adultery (Mark 6:14–29). "What a ruler does privately is none of your business."

CROSSING THE BOUNDARIES

There is always the danger of jurisdictional usurpation when civil government removes the jurisdictional boundaries and enters the domain of the Church. The Bible cites several examples of how the king sought to overrule the authority and jurisdiction of the Church. King Saul assumed the duties of the priests when he offered sacrifices. He stepped out of bounds from his kingly duties (1 Sam. 15:9–15, 22).

King Jeroboam established his State religion in Bethel and Dan. Non-Levites of the worst character were appointed to serve as priests (1 Kings 12:26–31).

Then there's the incident of King Uzziah who crossed the boundary in a seemingly minor way but was judged harshly. God is serious about jurisdictional church-state separation. The king is said to have been "proud" (2 Chron. 26:16). His pride led him to go beyond his legitimate civil jurisdiction and move into the ecclesiastical area. While he was "chief of State," being the king in Judah, he was not a priest. King Uzziah could not assume the role of a priest and perform in the most basic ecclesiastical duties. He had no jurisdictional authority to serve in the Temple, the Old Testament equivalent of the New Testament Church. Uzziah ignored God's law and "acted corruptly, and he was unfaithful to the LORD his God, for he entered the temple of the LORD to burn incense on the altar of incense" (2 Chron. 26:16).

The king was struck with the most feared disease in all Israel: leprosy! "And king Uzziah was a leper to the day of his death; and he lived in a separate house, being a leper, for he was cut off from the house of the LORD" (v. 21). He lost access to the Temple, was isolated from the general population, and lost his kingdom to his son, Jotham, who "was over the king's house judging the people of the land" (v. 21).

Azariah the priest was not passive in this incident. He knew the limitations of the king's power. He, along with "eighty priests of the LORD" (v. 17), took action against the king. They "opposed Uzziah the king" (v. 18), making it clear that "it is not for you, Uzziah, to burn incense to the LORD, but for the priests, the sons of Aaron who are consecrated to burn incense" (v. 18). The priests commanded Uzziah to "get out of the sanctuary" (v. 18).

These "ecclesiastical officials" are called "valiant men" (v. 17) because they acted with great risk. While there were eighty of them, the king still commanded an army. He could have put them to death.

There was a precedent for this when Ahimelech the priest helped David against King Saul (1 Sam. 21–22). Saul called on Doeg the Edomite to attack the priests after the king's own servants refused: "And Doeg the Edomite turned around and attacked the priests, and he killed that day eighty-five who wore the linen ephod" (1 Sam. 22:18). Doeg the Edomite had no qualms about killing the priests. King Uzziah had Saul's hate in his eye: "Uzziah, with a censer in his hand for burning incense, was enraged" (2 Chron. 26:19).

There have been times when the Church has forgotten its God-ordained jurisdictional role. The Church can deny its prophetic ministry when it is seduced by politics, that is, seeing politics as the sole way to advance God's kingdom. Isn't this what happened when the people wanted to crown Jesus as King, to make Him their political ruler? (John 6:15). They showed their true allegiance when Jesus refused to accept their view of what they thought God's kingdom should be like. "The distribution of bread moved the crowd to acclaim Jesus as the New Moses, the provider, the Welfare King whom they had been waiting for."[1]

When Jesus did not satisfy the false conception of salvation, some turned elsewhere and cried out: "We have no king but Caesar" (John 19:15). They denied the transforming work of the Holy Spirit to regenerate the dead heart of man. For them and for many today, human salvation comes through political power. Jesus is not a political savior, but His saving work should impact politics, because civil government is ordained by God.

THE FIRST AMENDMENT TO THE CONSTITUTION

Christianity and the Constitution

Does the First Amendment require a secular government? Is the First Amendment violated when Christians apply biblical principles to public policy issues? Too many debates over the meaning of the First Amendment are confused by a failure to

---

1. John Howard Yoder, *The Politics of Jesus: Vicit Agnus Noster* (Grand Rapids, MI: Eerdmans, 1972), 42.

cite it accurately or comprehensively: "Congress shall make no law respecting an establishment of religion, or prohibiting the free exercise thereof; or abridging the freedom of speech or of the press; or the right of the people peaceably to assemble, and to petition the Government for a redress of grievances."

An accurate interpretation of the amendment must include the following:

- There is no mention of the words Church, State, or Separation in the First Amendment.

- Included in the amendment are additional rights which relate to the free exercise of religion: the right to talk about religion (freedom of speech), the right to publish religious works (freedom of the press), the right of people to worship publicly, either individually or in groups (freedom of assembly), and the right to petition the government when it goes beyond its delegated constitutional authority in these areas (the right of political discourse and participation).

- The prohibition in the First Amendment is addressed exclusively to *Congress*. Individual states and governmental institutions (e.g., public schools, Capitol building steps, national parks, etc.) are not included in the amendment's prohibition. As clear as this is, some try to rewrite the First Amendment to fit their misconceptions about its meaning and implementation. One way is to make the amendment apply to the states, as in this example: "The First Amendment to the U.S. Constitution is the direct descendant of Jefferson's Virginia resolution, and its words are quite clear. Congress, *and by extension the states*, 'shall make no law respecting an establishment of religion.'"² If the constitutional framers wanted to include the phrase "and by extension the states," they would have done so. Since the states insisted on including a Bill of Rights to protect their civil jurisdictions, why would they include an amendment that restricted their sovereignty?

- There is no mention of a freedom *from* religion. The First Amendment offers no support of a position that would outlaw religion just because it exists or offends those of a different religion or those who have no religion at all.

- There is a second part to the religion clause of the First Amendment that states that Congress cannot "prohibit the free exercise thereof." In a June 19, 2000, ruling by the Supreme Court, the majority of justices outlawed student-led prayer at high school sporting events. For example, a teacher of political science and constitutional law at Agnes Scott College in Decatur, Georgia, in support of the Court's decision, never quotes the clause that mandates that there can be *no prohibition* of "the free exercise of religion."³

With so much debate, how does anyone know what the First Amendment means? An interpreter of any document as important as the Constitution must consider the historical circumstances that led to its formation, the vocabulary of the period, documents of similar construction, the political views of the

---

2. Editorial Page, *Atlanta Constitution* (November 15, 1994), A18.

3. Gus Cochran, "Court rightfully tosses prayers," *Atlanta Constitution* (June 20, 2000), A9.

authors, the prevailing religious worldview, and the intended audience. With these points in mind, it would be wise, therefore, to follow the method suggested by Thomas Jefferson in understanding the *original meaning* of the First Amendment:

> On every question of construction, carry ourselves back to the
> time when the constitution was adopted, recollect the spirit
> manifested in the debates, and instead of trying what meaning
> may be squeezed out of the text, or invented against it, con-
> form to the probable one in which it was passed.[4]

James Wilson (1742–1798) offered similar sound advice. "The first and governing maxim in the interpretation of a statute is to discover the meaning of those who made it." As Oliver Wendell Holmes put it, "A page of history is worth a volume of logic."[5]

The Amendment's History

With this brief introduction, let's look into the history behind this much referred to but often misquoted, misunderstood, and misapplied amendment. When the Constitution was sent to the states for ratification, there was fear that the new national government had too much power. It was proposed that prohibitions should be listed in the Constitution to restrict further the national government's power and authority.

---

4. Letter to Justice William Johnson, Monticello, June 12, 1823. See Thomas Jefferson, *Thomas Jefferson: Writings (Autobiography, Notes on the State of Virginia, Public and Private Papers, Addresses, Letters)* (New York: The Library of America, 1984), 1475

5. *New York Trust Co. v. Eisner*, 256 U.S. 345, 349 (1921). Quoted in Daniel L. Dreisbach, *Real Threat and Mere Shadow: Religious Liberty and the First Amendment* (Westchester, IL: Crossway Books, 1987), xiii.

Some of the framers were concerned that the federal government would establish a *national* Church (e.g., Anglican, Presbyterian, or Congregational) to be funded by tax dollars and controlled by the newly formed government, and that a national Church would disestablish the existing churches at the state level. So then, the First Amendment was designed to protect the *states* against the national (federal) government. The amendment was not designed to disestablish the Christian religion as it found expression in some of the state constitutions or anywhere else. Justice Joseph Story, a Supreme Court justice of the nineteenth century, offers the following commentary on the amendment's original meaning:

> The real object of the First Amendment was not to countenance, much less to advance Mohammedanism, or Judaism, or infidelity, by prostrating Christianity, but to exclude all rivalry among Christian sects [denominations] and to prevent any national ecclesiastical establishment which would give to an hierarchy the exclusive patronage of the national government.[6]

Story's comments are important. He states that the amendment's purpose was "to exclude all rivalry among *Christian* sects," that is, denominations. This assessment presupposes that Christianity was the accepted religion of the colonies but that no single sect should be mandated by law. The amendment was not designed to make all religions equal, but only to make all *Christian* denominations (sects) equal in the eyes of the Constitution and the law.

---

6. Quoted by Judge Brevard Hand, in *Jaffree vs. Board of School Commissioners of Mobile County*, 544 F. Supp. 1104 (S. D. Ala. 1983) in Russell Kirk, ed., *The Assault on Religion: Commentaries on the Decline of Religious Liberty* (Lanham, NY: University Press of America, 1986), 84.

The Establishment Clause

The word "establishment," as used in the First Amendment, means recognition by civil government of a single denomination as the official State Church. The amendment does not prohibit *the* establishment of religion in general, but rather *an* establishment of a particular Christian denomination, which our founders called a "sect." Furthermore, there is nothing in the First Amendment restricting the states. The restriction only applies to Congress, our nation's law-making body: "*Congress* shall make no law...." Writing the minority opinion in the *Wallace vs. Jaffree* case (1985), Supreme Court Justice William Rehnquist stated, "The Framers intended the Establishment Clause to prohibit the designation of any church as a 'national' one. The clause was also designed to stop the Federal government from asserting a preference for one religious denomination or sect over others."[7]

If the amendment had been constructed to remove religion from having an impact on civil governmental issues, then it would seem rather strange that on September 24, 1789, the same day that it approved the First Amendment, Congress called on President Washington to proclaim a National Day of Prayer and thanksgiving which read:

> That a joint committee of both Houses be directed to wait upon the President of the United States to request that he would recommend to the people of the United States a day of public thanksgiving and prayer, to be observed by acknowledging, with grateful hearts, the many signal favors of Almighty God, espe-

---

7. *Wallace v. Jaffree*, 472 U.S., 113. Jude P. Dougherty, "Separating Church and State," *The World & I* (December 1987), 686.

cially by affording them an opportunity peaceably to establish a Constitution of government for their safety and happiness.[8]

This proclamation acknowledges "the many signal favors of Almighty God, especially by *affording them an opportunity peaceably to establish a Constitution of government for their safety and happiness.*" This is odd language for a group of men who supposedly just separated religion from government at all levels. In fact, this resolution uses devoutly religious language to acknowledge that they would not have a government without God's blessing.

Historical Fiction

The origin of the "separation between Church and State" phrase has two sources. The first is in the writings of Roger Williams, founder of Rhode Island. The most noted reference, however, is a letter Thomas Jefferson wrote to a group of Baptist pastors in Danbury, Connecticut, in 1802. In that letter Jefferson wrote:

> Believing with you that religion is a matter which lies solely between man and his God, that he owes account to none other for faith or his worship, that the legislative powers of government reach actions only, and not opinions, I contemplate with sovereign reverence that act of the whole American people which declared that their legislature should "make no law respecting an establishment of religion, or prohibiting the free exercise thereof," thus building a wall of separation between church and state.[9]

---

8. *The Annals of the Congress, The Debates and Proceedings in the Congress of the United States*, Compiled From Authentic Materials by Joseph Gales, Senior (Washington, DC: Gales and Seaton, 1834), 1:949–50.

9. Quoted in Charles E. Rice, *The Supreme Court and Public Prayer: The Need for Restraint* (New York: Fordham University Press, 1964), 63.

Jefferson had no hand in the drafting of the Constitution or the Bill of Rights. He was in France at the time. While Jefferson's opinions are instructive, they remain opinions. His personal correspondence, even as President, has no legal standing. In addition, Jefferson's use of the phrase "separation between church and state" is "a mere metaphor too vague to support any theory of the Establishment Clause."[10] Yet, it is Jefferson's vague "metaphor" that has been adopted as the standard substitute for the actual language of the First Amendment.

When he was governor of Virginia, Jefferson readily issued proclamations declaring days of "public and solemn thanksgiving and prayer to Almighty God."[11] Jefferson's Virginia "Bill for Punishing Disturbers of Religious Worship and Sabbath Breakers" was introduced by James Madison in the Virginia Assembly in 1785 and became law in 1786. The section on Sabbath desecration reads:

> If any person on Sunday shall himself be found labouring at his own or any other trade or calling, or shall employ his apprentices, servants or slaves in labour, or other business, except it be in the ordinary household offices of daily necessity, or other work of necessity or charity, he shall forfeit the sum of ten shillings for every such offence, deeming every apprentice, servant, or slave so employed, and every day he shall be so employed as constituting a distinct offence.[12]

---

10. Peter J. Ferrara, *Religion and the Constitution: A Reinterpretation* (Washington, DC: Free Congress Foundation, 1983), 3435.

11. Quoted in Rice, *The Supreme Court and Public Prayer*, 63.

12. *The Papers of Thomas Jefferson*, "A Bill for Punishing Disturbers of Religious Worship and Sabbath Breakers," in Julian P. Boyd, ed. (Princeton, NJ: Princeton University Press, 1950), Vol. 2, 1777 to June 18, 1779, Including the Revisal of the Laws, 1776–1786, 555. Robert L. Cord, *Separation of Church and*

As president, Jefferson included a prayer in each of his two inaugural addresses. He signed bills appropriating money for chaplains in Congress and the armed services, and signed the Articles of War, which not only provided for chaplains but also "earnestly recommended to all officers and soldiers, diligently to attend divine services."[13]

In his Second Inaugural Address (1805), Jefferson stated, "In matters of religion I have considered that its free exercise is placed by the Constitution independent of the powers of the General Government. I have therefore undertaken on no occasion to prescribe the religious exercises suited to it, but have left them, as the Constitution found them, under the direction and discipline of the church or state authorities acknowledged by the several religious societies."[14] According to Jefferson, the federal ("General") Government has no jurisdiction over churches or state governments. "Many contemporary writers attempt to read back into the past a 'wall of separation' between church and state which in fact never has existed in the United States."[15]

Constitutional scholar Leo Pfeffer writes, "[F]or all practical purposes Christianity and religion were synonymous."[16] Our founders never supposed that moral precepts founded on the

---

State: Historical Fact and Current Fiction (Grand Rapids, MI: Baker Book House, [1982] 1988), 217.

13. Act of April 10, 1806, C. 20, 2 Stat. 359, 360. Quoted in Rice, *The Supreme Court and Public Prayer*, 6364.

14. Thomas Jefferson, "Second Inaugural Address," in James D. Richardson, ed., *A Compilation of the Messages and Papers of the Presidents, 1789–1902*, 12 vols. (Washington, DC: Bureau of National Literature and Art, 1907), 1:379–380.

15. Franklin Hamlin Littell, *From State Church to Pluralism: A Protestant Interpretation of Religion in American History* (Chicago, IL: Aldine Publishing Co., 1962), 99.

16. Leo Pfeffer, *Church, State and Freedom* (Boston, MA: Beacon Press, 1953), 98.

Christian religion should be excluded from policy making even though they worked diligently to keep the institutions and jurisdictions of Church and State separate.

All fifty state constitutions mention God using various designations such as "Supreme Ruler of the Universe," "Creator," "God," "Divine Goodness," "Divine Guidance," "Supreme Being," "Lord," "Sovereign Ruler of the Universe," "Legislator of the Universe," with "Almighty God" as the most common biblical phrase (Gen. 17:1; 28:3; 35:11; 43:14; 48:3; etc.).

The Declaration of Independence points out that our rights are an endowment from our "Creator" from whom we get certain "inalienable" rights, that is, rights that cannot be taken away from or given away by the possessor. There is even an appeal to the "Supreme Judge of the world" and "with a firm reliance on the protection of divine Providence."

The Constitution ends with "Done in the Year of Our Lord...," a clear reference to the birth of Jesus Christ, and sets Sunday aside as a day of rest for the President (Article I, Section 7). Two chaplains were appointed to Congress, one to the House of Representatives and one to the Senate, with an annual salary of $500 each, with no thought of violating the Constitution.

On March 16, 1776, "by order of Congress" a "day of Humiliation, Fasting and Prayer" was instituted and the people of the nation were called on to **acknowledge the over ruling providence of God**" and bewail their "**manifold sins and transgressions**, and, by a sincere repentance and amendment of life, appease his righteous displeasure, and, **through the merits and mediation of Jesus Christ**, obtain his pardon and forgiveness."[17]

---

17. Original document can be viewed at https://bit.ly/3mFdTTF

Congress set aside December 18, 1777 as a day of thanksgiving so the people could "express the grateful feelings of their hearts and consecrate themselves to the service of their divine benefactor"[18] and "join the penitent confession of their manifold sins...that it may please God, **through the merits of Jesus Christ**, mercifully to forgive and blot them out of remembrance." Congress also recommended that they petition God "to prosper the means of religion for the promotion and enlargement of that kingdom which consists in righteousness, **peace and joy in the Holy Ghost.**"[19]

It has been reported that on April 30, 1789 that George Washington took the oath of office with his hand on an open Bible and said after taking the oath, "I swear, so help me God." Following Washington's example, presidents still invoke God's name in their swearing-in ceremony.[20] The inauguration was followed by "divine services" held in St. Paul's Chapel, "performed by the Chaplain of Congress."[21]

CONCLUSION

The First Amendment "provides a *legal* separation between Church and State: *not a moral nor a spiritual* separation.... There is no reason, under the Constitution of the United States, why

---

18. In another context, "divine benefactor" would be viewed as a deist ascription to an unnamed deity. It's obvious that in this context the Christian God is in view.

19. A copy of the original document can be viewed at https://bit.ly/3mF-dTTF. The proclamation can also be seen in Gary DeMar, *America's Christian History: The Untold Story* (Powder Springs, GA: American Vision, 2005), 252.

20. Richard G. Hutcheson, Jr., *God in the White House: How Religion Has Changed the Modern Presidency* (New York: Macmillan, 1988), 37.

21. Anson Phelps Stokes and Leo Pfeffer, *Church and State in the United States*, one-volume ed. (New York: Harper & Row, 1964), 87.

the principles of Christianity cannot pervade the laws and institutions of the United States of America."[22] Today's Christian political activists are not calling on the State to establish churches, to force people to attend church, or to pay for the work of the church. They are simply maintaining that we cannot have good government without a moral foundation and that moral foundation resides in the Christian religion.

Greg Bahnsen explains the biblical model even during Israel's theocracy:

> [T]he Mosaic law provided the same protections for the circumcised Jew as for the uncircumcised stranger in Israel (e.g., Ex. 12:49; Lev. 24:22; Num. 15:16); the circumcised Jew who refused to follow the religious ritual might be excommunicated (Num. 9:13), but the uncircumcised stranger was free to submit to the religious ceremonies (Num. 9:1; 15:14) or to choose not to do so without civil penalty. The civil magistrate was not authorized, nor were sanctions specified, in the law of Moses to judge the unbelief of one's heart.[23]

Unlike a religion like Islam, Christianity does not force compliance to the Christian faith. No one is forced to accept Jesus as Savior and Lord or to attend religious services. There is no civil penalty for rejecting the Christian faith.

---

22. J. Marcellus Kik, *Church and State* (Nashville: Thomas Nelson, 1963), 116.

23. Greg L. Bahnsen, *No Other Standard: Theonomy and Its Critics* (Tyler, TX: Institute for Christian Economics, 1991), 187.

8

The "Jesus Was a Socialist" and "Property is Theft" Lies

"You shall not steal" is a fundamental biblical commandment that's found in both Testaments (Ex. 20:15; 21:16; Lev. 19:11, 13; Matt. 19:18; Rom. 13:9). If property is theft, as is often claimed, then every person in the world is a thief because everyone owns something.

Property rights were fundamental in the Bible, so much so that they've been written into our nation's laws:

> Iron pins are a common and useful means of identifying property corners and they and other similar monuments serve a useful purpose. The installation and maintenance of permanent monuments identifying land corners even preserves the good order of society itself. From earliest times the law not only authorized but protected landmarks. Interference with landmarks of another was a violation of the Mosaic law. See Deuteronomy 19:14; 27:17; Job 24:2; Proverbs 22:28; 23:10.

(256 Ga. 54, *International Paper Realty Company v. Bethune.* No. 43092. Supreme Court of Georgia, June 10, 1986).

In a list of those who do evil, the book of Job includes those who "remove the landmarks" and thereby "seize and devour flocks" (24:2).

In 1 Kings 21, we read the story of the prophet Elijah who rebuked Ahab and Jezebel for the murder of Naboth and their theft of his vineyard. Did Elijah say that this was a way to achieve economic equality by diminishing the wealth of some for the benefit of others? He pronounced severe judgment on Ahab and Jezebel for their theft.

If property is theft and civil governments take property from some people and give it to other people, then these governments are guilty of theft by holding the property and giving it to other people. The people receiving the property would now be guilty of theft by receiving property, which is theft.

In addition to a specific commandment not to steal, there is the commandment not to covet:

"You shall not covet your neighbor's house; you shall not covet your neighbor's wife or his male servant or his female servant or his ox or his donkey or anything that belongs to your neighbor" (Ex. 20:17). Covetousness is not just a sin of the wealthy. Anyone can covet. This includes the poor and governments that promise benefits to the people by promising to take from some so it can be given to others to secure their vote.

Thomas Sowell writes, "I have never understood why it is 'greed' to want to keep the money you have earned but *not* greed to want to take somebody else's money."[1]

---

1. Thomas Sowell, *Barbarians Inside the Gates and Other Controversial Essays*

LAWS AGAINST THEFT AND
COVETOUSNESS STILL APPLY

One of the most bizarre arguments for "Jesus was a socialist" comes from people who say, "Jesus healed and fed people for free; therefore, He was a socialist." When governments can feed people for free by multiplying loaves and fishes, heal people by touch or a word from a government agency, or raise people from the dead, then I'll become a socialist. The thing of it is, people who want free college and free healthcare and politicians who promise such things believe that government is god and can turn stones into bread. Our nation's motto is "In God We Trust" which means in practice "In Government We Trust." As often as they try, governments can't perform miracles.

I consistently read from some Christians that under the New Covenant believers aren't bound by God's commandments, even though the New Testament says we are: "For this is the love of God, that we keep His commandments; and His commandments are not burdensome" (1 John 5:3; John 14:15; 15:10; 1 John 2:3; 3:22, 24; Rev. 12:17; 14:12). It's true that laws related to animal sacrifices are done away with in the person and work of Jesus Christ. He is the "lamb of God" (John 1:29), the temple made without hands (2:13–25), and the sinless high priest (Heb. 7).

The moral law as it relates to covetousness and theft has not been abolished. The apostle Paul writes:

> What shall we say then? Is the Law sin? May it never be! On the
> contrary, I would not have come to know sin except through
> the Law; for I would not have known about coveting if the Law

(Stanford, CA: Hoover Institution Press Publication, 1999).

had not said, "You shall not covet." But sin, taking opportunity through the commandment, produced in me coveting of every kind; for apart from the Law sin is dead. I was once alive apart from the Law; but when the commandment came, sin became alive and I died; and this commandment, which was to result in life, proved to result in death for me; for sin, taking an opportunity through the commandment, deceived me and through it killed me. So then, **the Law is holy, and the commandment is holy and righteous and good** (Rom. 7:7–12).

The commandments tell us when we are sinning. We have been freed from the curse of the law but not from obeying the law, because the law is good (Rom. 7:12, 16; 1 Tim. 1:8). If the moral law is done away with, then there is no such thing as stealing and it's okay for the government and anyone else to take money from some people so it can be given to other people.

Paul writes, "He who steals must steal no longer; but rather he must labor, performing with his own hands what is good, so that he will have something to share with one who has need" (Eph. 4:28). How can Paul tell someone not to steal if the commandments have been done away with? It's not only wrong for individuals to steal, but it's wrong for governments to steal.

Socialism is theft; it's the transfer of wealth from some people so it can be given to other people by force with the promise that wealth will be equalized. Socialism creates a ruling class that enriches itself in the name of the people and the promise of income equality. These rulers are government thieves, like the rich young ruler (Luke 18:18) and the rich chief tax collector Zacchaeus (Luke 19:1–10) who worked for the Roman State to help the rulers steal from his fellow Jews to empower the Empire.

EMPOWERING THE STATE

The story of the rich young ruler is not about socialism (Mark 10:17–27). It's possible that the rich ruler had inherited his title and fortune through fraud and political connections (Mark 10:19). Jerry Bowyer comments:

> [The power structure] involves the use of corrupt magistrates (who also often served on the same Sanhedrin on which the rich, young archon [ruler] would have served). The lawyers, whom Jesus strongly denounced, had developed numerous tricks by which to defraud the poor in favor of the nobility. That seems to be the "defrauding" to which Jesus and his younger brother James [James 2:6] referred when confronting the Jerusalem elites.[2]

Socialism is the same in the name of "social justice" by using civil government as a means to justice that ends up enriching those who wield power and gain power for themselves. Why was it wrong for Zacchaeus to defraud and not the civil government? Jesus didn't use the example of the rich man strangled by his wealth to appeal to Rome to tax the rich so the poor will benefit. "He was a ruler, a man of the state." It is odd, Bowyer writes, "to see people who want to increase the power of rulers invoke Jesus' commentary against a ruler." If Jesus' objective was to use the power of the civil magistrate to equalize wealth, then why didn't He object to Joseph of Arimathea who is described as a "rich man" (Matt. 27:57; Mark 15:43)? If Jesus hated the rich, why didn't he condemn Joseph? Why did God enrich Abraham (Gen. 13:2) and Job (Job 42:12)?

---

2. Jerry Bowyer, "Jesus vs. The Rich Senator," Townhall Finance (Sept. 17, 2018): https://bit.ly/2M8oEwU

It's true that Jesus said that we should care for "the least of these" (Matt. 25:40). Who are the "these"? The context makes it clear that Jesus limits the scope to "these brothers of Mine." This does not mean that we should no help other people; it does mean that charity is best given to those we know with the goal to make them less dependent on charity. Keep in mind that financial support given by civil government is not charity since the money given to some people was first taken by force from other people.

Note that there is no mention of government programs, legislation, or mandates in what Jesus says. The directive is aimed at individuals, not faceless and nameless bureaucrats. Rome had the power to tax (Luke 2:1; Matt. 22:15–22), and yet Jesus never petitions the Empire to force people to pay their "fair share" in the development of a welfare State. Jesus believed in limited government.

The Good Samaritan is an example of how aid should be handled. The Samaritan took care of the "half dead" man out of his own pocket. He "bandaged up his wounds, pouring oil and wine on *them;* and he put him on his own beast, and brought him to an inn." And "the next day he took out two denarii and gave them to the innkeeper and said, 'Take care of him; and whatever more you spend, when I return, I will repay you'" (Luke 10:30–37).

THE BIBLICAL WORK ETHIC

The apostle Paul commanded that those who did not work should not eat (2 Thess. 3:10; also, 1 Thess. 4:11). Gleaning in the Old Testament was a way to help the poor. Even the poorest members of society had to work (Lev. 19:9–10; 23:22; Deut. 24:20–22). Jesus and His disciples practiced a form of gleaning as they walked through grain fields breaking off heads of wheat to eat (Mark 2:23). Gleaning was hard work, and it was not a government program. If people of means didn't have the fields that could be gleaned, there wouldn't be anything to glean.

In the film *The Boy Who Harnessed the Wind*, a Malawian boy named William Kamkwamba (played by Maxwell Simba) saves his village from famine by constructing a windmill to provide water and electricity. All the parts for the windmill had been used and discarded—from the bicycle wheel and light to the truck battery and water pump. In a TED talk the 14-year-old gave in 2007, "he explained that since he couldn't afford his education, he dropped out of school. He found a book in the library called *Using Energy* that sparked the idea of creating the windmill. The book gave instructions on how to construct one, but Kamkwamba had to get creative with the materials he used."

He gleaned the materials to make what he needed. He couldn't glean what was not first produced by someone else.

Appeal cannot legitimately be made to Acts 2:44–45 and 4:32–37. These early Christians **voluntarily** sold their property and used the proceeds to help those in need. Neither the Empire nor the Church mandated that the property owners sell their property. Paul Solman, a business and economics correspondent for the PBS NewsHour, gets it wrong when he writes, "If you're looking for an apparent champion of pure collectivism, I suggest the evangelist Luke and his account of the first Christian Pentecost in Acts of the Apostles, 4:32 through 5:10."[3]

---

3. "Communism, Capitalism and the Third Thanksgiving" (November 22, 2012): https://to.pbs.org/3hPkIyD

Rousas J. Rushdoony puts the events in their proper historical context:

> The "communism" of the early church, in Acts, was not economic in any sense, and should not be considered as an economic experiment. The church took seriously our Lord's prophecy concerning the coming fall of Jerusalem (Matthew 24). They knew that they were living in a doomed city and country. The logical step of faith was to make liquid their assets for ready flight. Some who made liquid their assets dedicated their funds in part or whole to the church, for the evangelization of Judea before its destruction [Luke 21:20–24].
>
> The relief money collected by Paul was not collected because an economic experiment had failed at Jerusalem and Judea. Men there continued in their vocations, simply living in rented properties, since their assets had been made liquid. The problem was a severe drought which had struck the entire area [Acts 11:28], creating a serious economic crisis and extreme shortages of food [Rom. 15:25–26; 1 Cor. 16:1–3]. This is a matter of historical record. Outside help was needed by virtually all in Judea, and the Christians were no exceptions. Thus, 'communism' had nothing to do with it, and did not exist in the early church. Because the Christians were prepared for ready flight by our Lord's words, and by reason of having divested themselves of properties, none lost their lives in the fateful war with Rome, A.D. 66–70."[4]

---

4. From a personal letter written by R. J. Rushdoony sent to John R. Richardson and cited in *Christian Economics: The Christian Message to the Market Place* (Houston: St. Thomas Press, 1966), 60.

There would not have been the ability to help their fellow Christians who were suffering from the effects of famine (Acts 11:28) if Communism was operating since there wouldn't have been any money to share. There wouldn't have been any property to make available to those in need.

If everyone had sold all their land and houses, where did they live? In the streets? They would not have been able to live with other Christians since, according to those who claim those in the early, also would have sold their land and houses. It's obvious that those in Jerusalem sold what they did not need to live so they could help those in immediate need. Maybe those in need were disinherited because they had deserted Judaism. Some may have lost their jobs.

THE COMING DOOM ON JERUSALEM

Also, as noted above, they had been warned by Jesus that Jerusalem would be destroyed before their generation passed away (Matt. 24:34). Christians still must have had houses in the lead up to the destruction of Jerusalem, otherwise why would Jesus have said, "Whoever is on the housetop must not go down to get the things out that are in his house" (24:17).

They knew their land would lose its value when Jerusalem was eventually surrounded by armies (Luke 21:20), although they did not know the day or the hour when that would take place (Matt. 24:36). John Gill comments:

> This was done by Jews, and by Jews only; who, when they embraced the Gospel of Christ, were informed that the destruc-

tion of their city, and nation, was at hand; and therefore they sold their estates beforehand, and put them to this use; which was necessary to be done, both for the support of the Gospel in Judea, and for the carrying and spreading of it among the Gentiles: but is not to be drawn into a precedent, or an example in after times; nor is ever any such thing proposed to the Christian churches, or exhorted to by any of the apostles.

Paul takes up a collection for the Jerusalem church "from the saints" to help fellow-Christians in need (1 Cor. 16:1–4; 2 Cor. 8:1–9:15; Rom 15:14–32). They gave "according to their ability, and beyond their ability, **of their own accord**" (2 Cor. 8:3).

Mary and Lydia owned houses (Acts 12:12; 16:40). So did Prisca and Aquila (Rom. 16:3, 5). There are other examples throughout the New Testament of Christians owning property. Paul argues that the eighth commandment forbidding stealing is part of what it means to love your neighbor as yourself (Rom. 13:9). Paul mentions thieves as those who will not inherit the kingdom of God (1 Cor. 6:9–10). He clearly states, "He who steals must steal no longer; but rather he must labor, performing with his own hands what is good, so that he will have something to share with one who has need" (Eph. 4:28).

There was no government intervention, no command to sell everything, no directive for the people to give up all their possessions. Peter makes it clear that at every point in the sale of the property it was theirs to do with as they decided. This is made clear in the Ananias and Sapphira story: "While it remained *unsold*, did it not remain your own? And after it was sold, was it not under your control?" (Acts 5:4). John R. Richardson writes:

> No one was forced into giving up his goods and possessions.
> It was not socialism legislated either by church or state. It does

not resemble modern communism in any respect. . . . Ananais was free to keep or sell his property. When he sold it, he had the right to determine whether he would give all of it, or part of it, or none of it, into the treasury of the church for the alleviation of the needs of poor Christians. J. W. Lipscomb is certainly correct when he says, "The program was a voluntary expression of Christian concern for the needs of fellow Christians, and was not a program for compulsory collectivism such as we hear advocated all too often today."[5]

THE FAILURE OF COLLECTIVISM

Attempts at a socialistic economic system have been repeatedly tried with abject failure. For example, the Pilgrims were initially organized as a collectivist society as mandated by contract by their sponsoring investors. No matter how much a person worked, everyone would get the same amount. It didn't take long for the less industrious to realize that their diminished labor would net them the same result as the most industrious.

William Bradford, the acting governor of Plymouth Colony, wrote the following in his first-hand history of events in *Of Plymouth Plantation*:

> The experience that we had in this common course and condition [that was] tried sundry years . . . by taking away property, and bringing community into a commonwealth, would make them happy and flourishing—as if they were wiser than God.
>
> For this community (so far as it was) was found to breed much confusion and discontent and retard much employment

---

5. Richardson, *Christian Economics*, 60.

that would have been to their benefit and comfort. For young men that were most able and fit for labor and service did re-pine [express discontent] that they should spend their time and strength to work for other men's wives and children without [being paid] that was thought injustice.

What did Bradford do? "To rectify this situation, in 1623 Bradford abolished the socialism. He gave each household a par-cel of land and told them they could keep what they produced, or trade it away as they saw fit. In other words, he replaced socialism with a free market, and that was the end of the famines."[6]

The results were immediate and beneficial to all involved. "This [free enterprise] had very good success," Bradford wrote, "for it made all hands industrious, so as much more corn was planted than otherwise would have been."

Former Soviet leader Mikhail Gorbachev said the following in 1992: "Jesus was the first socialist, the first to seek a better life for mankind."[7] If Jesus was the first socialist, and socialism was for the betterment of mankind, then why is it that socialistic so-cieties are not a success? Why did the former Soviet Union aban-don its failed collectivist system? Why are controlled economies like North Korea, Venezuela, and Cuba failing economically?

Tyrannical regimes promise a better life. What tyrant ever says he will make things worse for people? Socialism has not created a better life for people. Economic liberty is based on the operating principle of "You shall not steal," even if it's by majority vote to promise free stuff to people who demand it. Supposedly, communism and socialism are about "sharing," and

6. Richard J. Maybury, "The Great Thanksgiving Hoax," Mises Daily Articles (Nov. 27, 2014): https://bit.ly/2ZTB7fc
7. London's *Daily Telegraph* (June 16, 1992).

many people are okay with that, even if it's at the point of a gun. For example, Brittany Griebling, a 35-year-old social worker, says socialism is "people making choices for themselves." No, Socialism is some people using the power and force of government to make choices for everyone using money taken from some people and given to other people.

Another said, "We're in an age where we can easily provide for everyone on the planet." Who are the "we" in this scenario? Socialism is forced compliance. If people decide to travel the world or engage in a year-long study of art, "we" should not be forced to pay for their aspirations.[8]

The history of Communism is a record of genocide,[9] as D. James Kennedy and Jerry Newcombe show in their book *What If Jesus Had Never Been Born?*:

> Mao killed about 72 million human beings from 1948 to 1976. When we add the 40 million Stalin is responsible for, we come to a number of 112 million. Throw in Hitler's 15 million (not counting the devastating war he started!), and we come to about 127 million. Add other killings by other atheistic and totalitarian states—as a result of their atheistic ideology—you come up with a number of more than 130 million.[10]

Alexander Solzhenitsyn's "estimates reach as high as sixty million" deaths just during Josef Stalin's reign of terror.[11] "His-

---

8. Holly Otterbein, "The Kids Are All Red: Socialism Rises Again in the Age of Trump," PhillyMag (Nov. 18, 2017): https://bit.ly/2zzLfQh

9. Mark Kramer, ed., *The Black Book of Communism: Crimes, Terror, Repression* (Cambridge, MA: Harvard University Press, 1997), 4.

10. D. James Kennedy and Jerry Newcombe, *What If Jesus Had Never Been Born?* (Nashville, TN: Thomas Nelson, 1994), 236.

11. Lloyd Billingsley, *The Generation that Knew Not Josef: A Critique of Marxism and the Religious Left* (Portland, OR: Multnomah Press, 1985), 38.

torian Robert Conquest, in *The Harvest of Sorrow*, his definitive account of Stalin's reign of rural terror, estimated that 14.4 million people, half of them children, perished."[12]

In addition to supporting an ideology that led to the deaths of tens of millions, today's misinformed hide behind the First Amendment in an attempt to make the case that governments should curtail economic freedom, a right that would not have been afforded to anyone who lived in any Communist nation.

---

12. Lewis Lord, "A reign of rural terror, a world away," *U.S. News & World Report* (June 30/July 7, 2003), 4.

9

Christian Involvement in Politics Under God's Government

Does the Bible forbid Christians from being involved in politics? It would be a hard case to prove since there are numerous books of the Bible that are filled with politics—from Joshua, Judges, and 1 and 2 Samuel to 1 and 2 Kings and the Old Testament Prophets.

King David is confronted by Nathan the Prophet (2 Sam. 12), Solomon is shown violating nearly every biblical admonition regarding kings, leading to his abandonment of the covenant (1 Kings 10–11), and kings are given direct instructions on what standard they should use in making decisions of a civil/political nature (Deut. 17), even to the point of not being mentally affected by wine or strong drink (Prov. 31:1–9). Early on, Moses is given instructions on the implementation of a decentralized civil system (Ex. 18).

In the New Testament, Israel was controlled by the Romans. Only Roman citizens had political standing (Acts 16:37; 22:25–29; 25:9–12). Jesus had a political trial because the Jews did not have the authority to put Him to death (John 18:30–31).[1] His accusers brought false civil charges against Him (Luke 23:1–2) to force Pilate's hand (John 19:12).

This is all to say that the conditions in Israel during the Roman occupation of Israel did not lend itself for non-Romans to influence the government. Over the centuries, however, Christianity impacted the civil sphere so that the citizenry had a voice in civil government. The development and signing of the Magna Carta (1215) are good examples of this principle.

Historian David Carpenter has written that the Great Charter "asserted a fundamental principle—the rule of law. The king was beneath the law, the law the Charter itself was making. He could no longer treat his subjects in an arbitrary fashion.... The Church in England was central to the development of legal and human rights centuries before the French Revolution... the first parties to the charter were the bishops—led by Stephen Langton of Canterbury, who was a major drafter and mediator between the king and the barons; and its first and last clauses state that 'the Church in England shall be free.'"[2]

The following are some reasons many Christians use to justify why they should not get involved culturally and politically:

---

1. "The Jews had lost this power since the time that Archelaus was deposed, and Judæa became a Roman province (AD 6 or 7). The Talmud speaks of the loss of this power forty years or more before the destruction of Jerusalem." This didn't stop the Jews from inflicting punishment without a trial (Acts 7:54–60; 14:19; 16:22; 2 Cor. 11:24–25

2. Eric Metaxas, "Why We Celebrate the Magna Carta," Christian Headlines (June 15, 2015): https://bit.ly/2UOiEhH

1. We should just preach the gospel: Paul told the Ephesian elders that he did not shrink from declaring to them the "whole purpose of God" (Acts 20:27). Being a new creature in Christ is the first step in a whole new life. Being born again does not stop at infancy. We are to grow up in the faith so every area of life is impacted by God's Word (Heb. 5:11–14). This includes politics, economics, law, education, journalism, ethics, and economics. The Bible has a great deal to say about all of these topics and much more.

2. Politics is dirty: What isn't dirty)? Our job is to clean up the things that are dirty. Diapers are dirty, and we change them. If a politician is dirty, then change him or her. If a policy is unbiblical or unconstitutional, oppose it and work for change. There's nothing in the Bible that says you can't involve yourself in the day-to-day decisions of life because people to bad things. If the government is instituting policies that hurt people, then we have a duty to oppose those implementing bad policies.

3. Jesus did not get mixed up in politics, so why should we?: There are many things Jesus didn't do. He didn't get married, have children, own a home (John 9:58), or have a means of transportation (Matt. 21:1–7). Should we follow His example in these areas? If you say that we shouldn't do what Jesus didn't do, then it's time you sold your home and car, stay single, and have no children.

4. Our citizenship is in heaven: We have multiple citizenships (commonwealths), with our heavenly citizenship being primary and a priority (Phil. 3:20; see Acts 5:29). Paul had multiple citizenships. He was a citizen of Israel and the tribe of Benjamin (Phil. 3:4; Rom. 11:1). The fact that Paul was a Hebrew citizen and a citizen of heaven did not stop him from claiming his Roman citizenship (Acts 16:37; 22:25–29) and appealing to Caesar (25:9–12) when he was under Rome's jurisdiction.

5. There's a separation between church and state: The Bible teaches that there is a jurisdictional separation between church and state, but there is no separation between God and governments (self-, family, church, and civil). The civil magistrate is said to be a "minister of God" (Rom. 13:1–4). It's the same Greek word (διάκονός/*diakonos*) used to describe a deacon in an ecclesiastical/church setting (1 Tim. 3:8–13). In neither of these government offices are these ministers to "lord it over those allotted to [their] charge" (1 Pet. 5:3). The First Amendment to the Constitution does not use the phrase "separation of church and state" (see Chapter 7). The prohibition is directed at the National Government not to establish a national religion: "Congress shall make no law respecting an establishment of religion or the free exercise thereof." The Amendment goes on to maintain that we are free to speak about religion, write about religion, congregate about religion and "petition the government for a redress of grievances." This means that we have the liberty to change the government, something that was not possible during the time of Jesus.

6. Jesus' kingdom is not of this world: God's kingdom does not derive its power and authority from this world, but His kingdom is in and over this world whether people acknowledge it or not. We are to pray, "Your kingdom come. Your will be done on earth as it is in heaven" (Matt. 7:10). Doing God's will is the manifestation of kingdom living.

7. Politics is not spiritual: If the civil government has been ordained by God, then it is spiritual, as is every area of life when governed by the Word of God. Being spiritual means being guided by the Holy Spirit; it does not mean floating in some upper story ethereal realm. Robert A. J. Gagnon wrote the following in a Facebook post, "Stop treating a masochistic desire for you and your children to be persecuted by the state as a mark of spirituality. Stop sleeping a Gethsemane sleep and passing it off as a Jesus-in-the-boat sleep. We know you have the 'innocent as doves' shtick down; now work on the 'wise as serpents' part."

Nineteenth-century theologian John Holt Rice (1777–1831), who opposed slavery and described it as "the greatest political evil which has ever entered the United States," opposed the church getting involved in its abolition through legislative means:

> The reason why I am so strenuously opposed to any move-ment by the church, or the ministers of religion on this subject, is simply this. I am convinced that anything we can do will in-jure religion, and retard the march of public feeling in relation to slavery. . . . Slaves by law are held as property. If the church or the minister of religion touches the subject, it is touching what are called the rights of property. The jealousy among our countrymen on this subject is such, that we cannot move a step in this way, without wakening up the strongest opposition, and producing the most violent excitement. The whole mass of the community will be set in motion, and the great body of the church will be carried along.
>
> Under this conviction, I wish the ministers of religion to be convinced that there is nothing in the New Testament which obliges them to take hold of this subject directly. In fact, I believe that it never has fared well with either church or state, when the church meddled with temporal affairs. And I

should—knowing how unmanageable religious feeling is when not kept under the immediate influence of divine truth—be exceedingly afraid to see it brought to bear *directly* on the subject of slavery. Where the movement might end, I could not pretend to conjecture.[3]

We don't have to conjecture. Rice's views, followed by many Christian leaders at the time and today, led to a bloody civil war where an estimated 620,000 men lost their lives, increased the power of the national government, and led to legal but immoral oppression of freed slaves.

7. Satan is the god of this world: Satan is no more a god than a person's stomach is a god (Phil. 3:19). Paul is describing what some people choose to be their god, a limited creature who has been defeated. The Greek word for "world" (*kosmos*) is not used; it's *aiōn* and refers to the time (lit., "age") when Jewish believers in Jesus were having to counter criticism from their fellow Jews over who Jesus was (1 John 2:18–19, 22; 2 John 7). Paul writes that these people were blinded (2 Cor. 3–4). Jesus said, "**Now** judgment is upon this world; **now** the ruler of this world will be cast out" (John 12:31; also, John 14:30; 16:11; 1 John 4:4; 5:19). Paul told the Christians in Rome, "The God of peace will **soon** crush Satan under your feet. The grace of our Lord Jesus be with you" (Rom 16:20). "Soon" for them.

8. We're not supposed to judge: We are admonished by Jesus to be consistent in judgment (Matt. 7:1–2) and to "judge with righteous judgment" (John 7:24). How can a Christian speak with a non-Christian about repentance if we aren't to

---

3. William Maxwell, *A Memoir of the Rev. John Holt Rice, D.D.* (Philadelphia: J. Whetham, 1835), 307.

judge in terms of God's moral standards? If there is nothing to judge, there is no sin and there is no need for the gospel. Paul certainly judged when it came to an inappropriate sexual relationship: "I, on my part, . . . have already **judged** him" (1 Cor 5:1–3). Every law is someone's view of moral judgment.

9. We must render to Caesar what is Caesar's: We don't live under Caesar. We live under a Constitution, and we can remove and replace people in office and "petition the government for a redress of grievances," as the First Amendment clearly states. The people in Jesus' day could not. We do not have to settle for the political status quo. In addition, Caesar (every civil government) must render to God what belongs to God. And what belongs to God? Everything!

10. Christians should remain neutral: Neutrality is impossible. Jesus said, "He who is not with Me is against Me; and he who does not gather with Me scatters" (Matt. 12:30). Those who refused to help the injured Samaritan were not being neutral (Luke 10:25–37). Those who cried out, "We have no king but Caesar" (John 19:15), were not being neutral. Pilate was not being neutral when he "washed his hands" (Matt. 27:24). Dr. Greg L. Bahnsen wrote:

> In addition to not having anything to speak before kings because of its endorsement of neutralism in civil affairs, the modern church has shown itself to be as antinomian in its theory of ethics as the autonomous secular man. As a result, the church fails to challenge "the powers that be" with the "power (authority)" of Christ or to offer restorative guidance to its society.

11. We can't impose our morality on other people: All law is the imposition of someone's view of morality. The question is, What areas of life are civil magistrates given the authority to legislate and by what ultimate standard? I can guarantee you that non-Christians have no problem imposing their morality on the rest of us. They do it with every piece of legislation they draft and hope to put into law.

12. It's never right to resist authority: The Hebrew midwives were commanded by "the king of Egypt" to put to death all the male children being born to the Hebrew women (Ex. 1:15–16). The Hebrew midwives disobeyed the edict of the king: "But the midwives feared God, and did not do as the king of Egypt had commanded them, but let the boys live" (1:17). The midwives had to make a choice. Did God's law overrule the command of a king, even "the king of Egypt"? God shows His approval of their actions: "So God was good to the midwives, and the people multiplied, and became very mighty. And it came about because the midwives feared God, that He established households for them" (1:20–21).

Rahab's misdirection to the Jericho authorities is another Old Testament example. Rahab is praised by two New Testament writers for her actions: "By faith Rahab the harlot did not perish along with those who were disobedient, after she had welcomed the spies in peace" (Heb. 11:31). Rahab is listed with Abraham as one whose faith was reflected in her works: "And in the same way [as Abraham] was not Rahab the harlot also justified by works, when she received the messengers and sent them out by another way?" (James 2:25). By sending the spies out by another way, she subverted the king's desire to capture the spies. In the New Testament, "Peter and John answered and said to [the authorities], 'Whether it is right in the sight of God to give heed to you rather than to God, you be the judge; for we cannot stop speaking about what we have seen and heard'" (Acts 4:19–20). Also, "We must obey God rather than men" (Acts 5:29).

13. We're living in the last days and Jesus is coming soon to rapture His church so why polish brass on a sinking ship?: How many times have we heard this claim? We were told in 1970 with the publication of Hal Lindsey's book *The Late Great Planet Earth* that the rapture would take place within forty years of Israel becoming a nation again (1948). Chuck Smith and others made the same claim: 1948 + 40 = 1988. Even today Christians are pushing the canard that the "rapture" is near, that the antichrist is on the brink of revealing himself, therefore, there is no reason to rearrange the deck chairs on the Ship of State since it's going to sink like the Titanic. Those in the world are wiser. Shipbuilding did not stop with the sinking of an un-sinkable ship. Sometimes "the sons of this age are more shrewd in relation to their own kind than the sons of light" (Luke 16:8).

BEING SALT AND LIGHT

There are other more nuanced reasons offered for non-involvement that sound super-spiritual. The following example is the article "The Salt of the Earth" written by Phil Johnson. Johnson begins his article by quoting the following verses:

> You are the salt of the earth.... You are the light of the world. ... Let your light shine before others, so that they may see your good works and give glory to your Father who is in heaven (Matt. 5:13–16).

Then he offers these comments:

That text is often cited as if it were a mandate for the church to engage in political activism—lobbying, rallying voters, organizing protests, and harnessing the evangelical movement for political clout. I recently heard a well-known evangelical leader say, "We need to make our voices heard in the voting booth, or we're not being salt and light the way Jesus commanded."

That view is pervasive. Say the phrase "salt and light," and the typical evangelical starts talking politics as if by Pavlovian reflex.

But look at Jesus' statement carefully in its context. He was not drumming up boycotts, protests, or a political campaign. He was calling His disciples to holy living.

Let's take Johnson's comment that Jesus was "calling His disciples to holy living." He makes a good point that all Christians can agree on. But where do we go to learn about holy living and how broad and comprehensive holy living is? Does it include politics, economics, raising children, church life, walking your dog, crossing the street, playing baseball, teaching a Sunday school class, pastoring a church, doing evangelism, creating music and art, developing a computer program?

Johnson can't say from the verses he quotes since Jesus doesn't give any details. Nothing is included or left out. Johnson is reading into verses things that aren't there. Or I should say that he is leaving out items that are found elsewhere in Scripture.

The writer to the Hebrews does something like what we read in Matthew 5. He tells his readers that by this point in their Christian walk they should be "teachers," but now they "need again for someone to teach [them] the elementary principles of the oracles of God," needing "milk and not solid food" (Heb.

5:12–13). He goes on to write that it's through practice that their senses are trained to "discern good and evil" (5:14). Like Jesus' words in the portion of the Sermon on the Mount that Johnson references, there are no particulars. There is no need for them, since earlier he wrote the following:

> For the word of God is living and active and sharper than any two-edged sword, and piercing as far as the division of soul and spirit, of both joints and marrow, and able to judge the thoughts and intentions of the heart (Heb. 4:12).

There is nothing in this passage that indicates that the realm of politics—civil government—is excluded since when the whole Bible is read, there is a great deal said about the subject of governmental politics. This is supported by the apostle Paul in his letter to Timothy:

> All Scripture is God-breathed and profitable for teaching, for reproof, for correction, for training in righteousness; that the man of God may be adequate, equipped for every good work (2 Tim. 3:16–17).

Of course, as we read on in the Sermon on the Mount (Matt. 5–7), Jesus mentions a number of moral particulars, but these three chapters do not exhaust what it means to live a holy life, especially when we read the above passages from Hebrews and 2 Timothy 3.

Why can't we shine the bright light of all of God's Word (Ps. 119:105) on the world—including civil government (described as "a minister of God": Rom. 13:1–7)—like we do for self-government ("self-control": Prov. 25:28), church government ("an overseer must be above reproach": 1 Tim. 3:2), business ("just weights and measures": Lev. 19:36), journalism ("do not bear false witness": Ex. 20:16), and everything else in life?

Consider these words from John MacArthur. I'm bringing MacArthur into the discussion because Johnson is the Executive Director of Grace to You, a Christian tape and radio ministry that features the preaching ministry of John MacArthur. Phil Johnson has been associated with MacArthur since 1981 and has edited some of MacArthur's major books. The following is from "You Are the Light of the World," a sermon that MacArthur preached on Matthew 5:14–16:

> I think God wants us to confront the world. Just because the world persecutes us, reviles us, and says all manner of evil against us falsely, just because it seems impossible that, in a country where the Constitution says no law could ever be passed that takes away any of the freedom of religion at all from anybody, we're facing the fact that you can't have a Bible study in your house without a permit. I really don't think that it will get any easier. I don't think that just because the world makes it tough on us that we should crawl in a hole or keep our mouths shut or hide. We should be like verse 13 [of Matthew 5], salt and light in the world.

MacArthur references the Constitution and notes that its original purpose was that "no law could ever be passed that takes away" anyone's freedom of religion. This seems to be a reference to the First Amendment. How did the First Amendment get into the Constitution? It was Christians who worked for it. They weren't satisfied with the text of the Constitution as it was drafted in 1787, so they pushed for a Bill of Rights to limit the power and authority of the newly constituted national civil government even more than the Constitution itself did.

In his battle with the state of California over indoor public worship because of prohibitions from civil officials over COVID-19, MacArthur has relied on the Bible and our written Constitution and its First Amendment protections to make his case.

The First Amendment is a political statement designed to keep Congress from interfering with religion at the state level. Following Johnson's logic, Christians who lobbied for a constitutional provision that "Congress shall make no law respecting an establishment of religion or prohibiting the free exercise thereof" were, to use his words, "lording it over" people, exercising "political dominion," and making "society righteous through legislation."

I suspect that most people would praise our Christian founders for putting into law the protections listed in the First Amendment to insure that churches can speak, write, and assemble about religion (all found in the amendment). That same First Amendment also gives citizens the right to "petition the government for a redress of grievances." Might not that include "boycotts, protests, or a political campaign"?

We're not subjects of Rome. "Render to Caesar the things that belong to Caesar" (Matt. 22:21) only applies to us in principle since we don't live under Caesar. If anything, the Constitution is our Caesar, and it gives us the right and responsibility to boycott, protest, campaign, and vote to change our government by changing those elected to office those who violate their sworn oath of office and legislate contrary to the Constitution.

People like Phil Johnson are living off borrowed capital. They denounce Christian involvement in politics but reap the benefits of generations of Christians that made it possible for them to enjoy the freedoms they have in this nation to preach the gospel unhindered. If we lose that freedom, it will be because Christians like Johnson and those who share his philosophy advise the church that to push for certain legislative remedies is an attempt to make "society righteous through legislation."

That's like saying working to pass a law to make buying and selling slaves illegal is an attempt to make society righteous through legislation. The purpose of the law is to protect people from being bought and sold like stolen cattle (Ex. 21:16; Deut. 24:7). Must we wait for the nation to become righteous before such a law is passed? Not according to the Bible:

> But we know that the Law is good, if one uses it lawfully, realizing the fact that law is not made for a righteous man, but for those who are lawless and rebellious, for the ungodly and sinners, for the unholy and profane, for those who kill their fathers or mothers, for murderers and immoral men and homosexuals and kidnappers and liars and perjurers, and whatever else is contrary to sound teaching, according to the glorious gospel of the blessed God, with which I have been entrusted (1 Tim. 1:8–11).

If everybody had to be righteous before a law was passed, we could never pass a law and slavery might still be legal. The passage and enforcement of laws keep most unrighteous people from acting out their unrighteousness because they know that painful sanctions are meted out for law breakers.

This is not to say that all immorality can be curtailed by passing laws or that there should be a law for every unrighteous deed. Even the Bible doesn't go that far. Prohibition is an example of trying to remedy a lack of self-control through legislation. By biblical standards, drunkenness is a sin (Prov. 20:1; 23:31–35;

Rom. 13:13; 1 Cor. 5:11; Eph. 5:18; 1 Thess. 5:7), but there is no call in the Bible to legislate against drinking alcohol.

Our duty as citizens is to see that civil government stays within its jurisdictional boundaries. This is exactly what Paul did when he questioned the authority of a civil official regarding his rights as a Roman citizen (Acts 22:23–30).

> But when [the Roman soldiers] stretched him out with thongs, Paul said to the centurion who was standing by, "Is it lawful for you to scourge a man who is a Roman and uncondemned?"

If it was right for Paul to "protest" this single violation of his rights as a Roman citizen, why is it wrong to protest constitutional violations given the fact the Constitution gives us the right to "petition the government for a redress of grievances"?

Phil Johnson is mismanaging the comprehensiveness of the Bible's message to speak to all of life by limiting the meaning of holy living to *personal* holiness. Holy living is not a narrow enterprise. It encompasses all of life.

PASTORS AND THE PULPIT

Several posts on Facebook asked this question: Should pastors address politics from the pulpit? I don't understand why this question keeps getting asked. If the Bible addresses politics (or anything else), then pastors must address politics and anything else the Bible addresses. It's that simple.

Are we to believe that in all the times the Bible has been preached or taught that the subject of politics should never come up? How does a minister preach and teach and not touch on the politics found, for example, in Exodus, Judges, 1 and

2 Samuel, 1 and 2 Kings, the prophets, and the politics of the
New Testament (e.g., Matt. 22:21; Acts 16:22–40; 22:22–30;
Rom. 13:1–4)?

Preachers and teachers are not to "shrink from declaring the
whole purpose of God" (Acts 20:27). If a topic is in the Bible, then pastors are obligated to preach on it. R. J. Rushdoony
wrote on this topic:

> What is the relation of clergy and politics? Should men in the
> pulpit speak out on social and political questions, and, if so,
> under what circumstances? Answer: The clergy cannot faith-
> fully expound the Word of God without dealing with virtually
> every social and political question. The Bible speaks not only
> about salvation but about God's law with respect to the state,
> money, land, natural resources, just weights and measures,
> criminal law, and a variety of other subjects. The clergy are not
> to intermeddle in politics, but they must proclaim the Word of
> God. There is a difference: political intermeddling is a concern
> over partisan issues: preaching should be concerned with Bib-
> lical doctrines irrespective of persons and parties.[4]

People ask why young people are leaving the church. In some
cases, it's because they don't see any real-world relevance. Yes, when
they die, they'll go to heaven, but what do they do until then? God
created the world and established its boundaries and rules for living in every area of life. The justice system we have today was at
some time largely based on biblical law. The laws that are being
overturned today for the most part are laws that Christians spent
centuries implementing. Let's tell young people about our history.

---

4. Rousas J. Rushdoony, *The Roots of Reconstruction* (Vallecito, CA: Ross
House Books, 1991), 552.

The late Chuck Colson described the time he spoke to the Texas legislature:

> I told them that the only answer to the crime problem is to take nonviolent criminals out of our prisons and make them pay back their victims with restitution. This is how we can solve the prison crowding problem.
>
> The amazing thing was that afterwards they came up to me one after another and said things like, "That's a tremendous idea. Why hasn't anyone thought of that?" I had the privilege of saying to them, "Read Exodus 22. It is only what God said to Moses on Mount Sinai thousands of years ago."[5]

If you want to get young people excited and motivated, teach them the whole purpose of God. Present the history of law in the world and how it has impacted the civilized world.

The Brett Kavanaugh Supreme Court hearings could serve as a great opportunity to address the subject of law, politics, and a whole lot more to young people. It would make a good sermon series on what the Bible says about jurisprudence. Such things are a major part of our lives. If pastors don't preach and teach on these topics, the people are going to go elsewhere for the information, much of which will be unreliable.

Joseph was put in prison because of the unsubstantiated testimony of one woman and what looked like a reliable piece of physical evidence—Joseph's garment that was left behind as he escaped (Gen. 39:12). She lied, and her political "privilege" gave her the upper hand. Biblical justice demands at least two witnesses.

---

5. Charles Colson, "The Kingdom of God and Human Kingdoms," *Transforming Our World: A Call to Action*, ed. James M. Boice (Portland, OR: Multnomah, 1988), 154–155).

- On the evidence of two witnesses or three witnesses, he who is to die shall be put to death; he shall not be put to death on the evidence of one witness (Deut. 17:6)
- A single witness shall not rise up against a man on account of any iniquity or any sin which he has committed; on the evidence of two or three witnesses a matter shall be confirmed (Deut. 19:15).
- But if he does not listen to you, take one or two more with you, so that BY THE MOUTH OF TWO OR THREE WITNESSES EVERY FACT MAY BE CONFIRMED (Matt. 18:16).
- This is the third time I am coming to you. EVERY FACT IS TO BE CONFIRMED BY THE TESTIMONY OF TWO OR THREE WITNESSES (2 Cor. 13:1).
- Do not receive an accusation against an elder except on the basis of two or three witnesses (1 Tim. 5:19).
- Even in your law it has been written that the testimony of two men is true (Heb. 10:28; also John 8:17).

Without eye-witness testimony, a confession, evaluation of evidence (Matt. 26:59; Acts 6:13)—physical or otherwise (Joshua 7:20 21)—reliability of testimonies (Mark 14:55–56), there is little a court of law can do. Parading supporters before a committee as "character references" or the use of raucous and threatening protests are not legitimate factors in adjudicating a case in terms of biblical norms.

So then, the Bible has much to say about these issues; it's long past time that we teach them from the pulpit so God's people will truly be salt and light.

10

Attempts to Rewrite
America's Christian History

After Mitt Romney's "Faith in America" speech delivered at the George Bush Presidential Library in College Station, Texas, on December 6, 2007,[1] Geoffrey Stone, professor of law at the University of Chicago, wrote that it "called to mind a disturbingly distorted version of history that has become part of the conventional wisdom of American politics in recent years."[2] Professor Stone separates the early founding of the nation (the Puritans) from its later incarnation of "the Founders."

If there was ever a distorted version of American history, it is Professor Stone's recounting of our nation's religious history in his article "Romney's Founders."[3] Part of the distortion comes because there is no neatly packaged history of the past. Like a wa-

---

1. https://n.pr/3fyF1zB

2. For a comprehensive contrary opinion, see Ellis Sandoz, ed., *Political Sermons of the American Founding: 1730—1805* (Indianapolis: LibertyPress, 1991).

3. Geoffrey R. Stone, "Romney's Founders," *The Huffington Post* (December 10, 2007): https://bit.ly/32qfzbT

termelon grown in a square bottle that takes the shape of its container,[4] historical summaries often take the shape of those doing the summarizing. To change the analogy, Stone, I believe, is engaged in a bit of historical trimming, selecting and "massaging" of the historical data to fit his own peculiar desired outcome.[5]

We're all susceptible to bending facts to fit our preconceptions. I'm not of the opinion that all our founders were Christians or that we were founded as a Christian nation in the official sense, although Supreme Court Justice David J. Brewer (1837–1910) attempted to make such a case.[6]

I do believe, however, that Christianity was woven into the warp and woof of our nation's foundational principles whether or not all those who drafted our nation's seminal documents were of an orthodox variety.

"GRATEFUL TO ALMIGHTY GOD"

Stone takes issue with the claim that "the founders intended to create a 'Christian nation,' and that we have unfortunately drifted away from that vision of the United States." Actually, the Founders inherited a nation founded by Christians and built on, to use a phrase from John Adams that appears in a letter written to Thomas Jefferson in 1813, "the general principles of Christianity" even though not every religious believer held to every tenet of Christian orthodoxy. Part of the problem with

---

4. http://bit.ly/Umihm

5. Walter Gratzer, *The Undergrowth of Science: Delusion, Self-Deception and Human Frailty* (Oxford, NY: Oxford University Press, 2000), vii.

6. See *Church of the Holy Trinity v. The United States* (143 United States 457), 1892 and David J. Brewer, *The United States: A Christian Nation* (Powder Springs, GA: American Vision, [1905] 1996).

Professor Stone's argument is that he views America's founding as a determined fixed point in time, and he picks the point most convenient for his argument. The colonists who created the first colonial governments that became the states that created the national government would object to the late-date founding of America. In fact, there are still remnants of that early religious founding circulating in documents, buildings, and ceremonies that organizations like the ACLU and Americans United for Separation of Church and State have made their living trying to eradicate.

There was a worldview prior to 1787 that did not pass into oblivion when the Constitution was finally ratified in 1791 with the added Bill of Rights. Many of the state constitutions were specifically Christian, and all were generally religious, an omission on Professor Stone's part of enormous significance. None of this changed with the ratification of the Constitution. In fact, today the fifty state constitutions mention God using various designations with "Supreme Ruler of the Universe," "Creator," "God," "Divine Goodness," "Divine Guidance," "Supreme Being," "Lord," "Sovereign Ruler of the Universe," "Legislator of the Universe," and "Almighty God" as the most common biblical phrase (Gen. 17:1; 28:3; 35:11; 43:14; 48:3; etc.). (The claim has been made that West Virginia is the exception. This is not the case.[7]) For example, the Preamble to the constitution of Professor Stone's home state of Illinois includes the following:

7. See "God in the State Constitutions": www.usconstitution.net/states_god.html. The West Virginia Preamble of 1872 reads, "Since through **Divine Providence** we enjoy the blessings of civil, political and religious liberty, we, the people of West Virginia reaffirm **our faith in and constant reliance upon God**." In 1960, the voters of the state of West Virginia ratified the following Preamble to their state's Constitution: "Since through **Divine Providence** we enjoy the blessings of civil, political and

We, the People of the State of Illinois—grateful to **Almighty God** for the civil, political and religious liberty which He has permitted us to enjoy and seeking **His blessing** upon our endeavors....

A number of state seals carry religious references. Here are some others:

Maryland
The State Seal pictured a farmer and a fisherman, reflecting the occupations of the early settlers; a shield with the coat of arms of the Calverts and the Crosslands (Alicia Crossland was the mother of the first Baron of Baltimore, George Calvert); and around the outer edge of the shield the Latin motto taken from the Latin Vulgate translation of the Bible: *Scuto Bonae Voluntatis Tuae Coronasti Nos*: "Thou hast crowned us with the shield of Thy good will" (Psalm 5:12).

Connecticut
Qui Transtulit Sustinet ("He Who Transplanted Still Sustains")

Florida
"In God We Trust."

Colorado
Nil Sine Numine ("Nothing without Providence")

South Dakota
"Under God the People Rule"

---

religious liberty, we, the people of West Virginia, in and through the provisions of this Constitution, reaffirm our faith in and **our constant reliance upon God**, and seek diligently to promote, preserve, and perpetuate good government in the State of West Virginia for the common welfare, freedom, and security of ourselves and our posterity." (Robert Bastress, *The West Virginia State Constitution* [Westport, CT: Greenwood Press, 1995], 27). The Preamble can be found at http://bit.ly/b43raK

Arizona

Originally adopted by the territory in 1863: *Ditat Deus* ("God Enriches")

Ohio

"With God All Things are Possible," from Matthew 19:26.

FAITH AND REASON

There is a long history of the relationship between the Christian religion and civil government in our nation. Professor Stone seems to place that relationship in the distant past as if our nation's Puritan forefathers were backwoods bumpkins who could hardly read or write and did not use reason. For one, Cotton Mather's (1663–1728) theological and scientific works made him famous around the world. "The University of Glasgow made him a Doctor of Divinity in 1710 and he became a Member of the Royal Academy in 1713." Mather supported the use of inoculation for smallpox. With this and so much more available to historians, Professor Stone is off-base with these comments:

> Those who promote this fiction confuse the Puritans, who intended to create a theocratic state, with the Founders, who lived 150 years later. The Founders were not Puritans, but men of the Enlightenment. They lived not in an Age of Faith, but in an Age of Reason. They viewed issues of religion through a prism of rational thought.

Space does not permit me to deal with his faith-reason dichotomy. Anyone having any background in Puritan studies knows it is absurd.[8] Reason was a tool, not the final arbiter of truth for the Puritans and their theological cousins, the Separatists who founded Plymouth Plantation in Massachusetts. Reason was valued because its source was God. Rodney Stark observes:

> As Quintus Tertullian instructed in the second century: "Reason is a thing of God, inasmuch as there is nothing which God the Maker of all has not provided, disposed, ordained by reason—nothing which He has not willed should be handled and understood by reason."

> Hence, Augustine merely expressed the prevailing wisdom when he held that reason was indispensable to faith: "Heaven forbid that God should hate in us that by which he made us superior to the animals! Heaven forbid that we should believe in such a way as not to accept or seek reasons, since we could not even believe if we did not possess rational souls."[9]

The reason-alone approach was displayed in all its raw consistency when the Enlightenment came full circle during the French Revolution when reason was made absolute and given god-like status. Heads literally rolled and blood flowed in the public squares. America's dance with the Enlightenment was held in check and overcome by the underlying moral tenets of Christianity. The Men of the Enlightenment did not reason autonomously as their reliance on and mention of God shows.

---

8. For starters, see John Morgan, *Godly Learning: Puritan Attitudes towards Reason, Learning and Education, 1560–1640* (New York: Cambridge University Press, 1986), chap. 3. A person who claims that reason is the ultimate standard must have a prior faith that reason is the ultimate standard. In addition, reasonable people disagree on what is reasonable.

9. Rodney Stark, *The Victory of Reason: How Christianity Led to Freedom, Capitalism, and Western Success* (New York: Random House, 2005), 7.

WHERE TO START

If we begin with 1620, the arrival of the Separatist Puritans at Plymouth, and add 150 years to that date, we come to 1770. Let's see if Professor Stone's thesis holds up. Beginning in 1774, Congress appointed chaplains for itself and the army. It sponsored the publication of a Bible. Christian morality was adopted by the armed forces, and public lands were made available to promote Christianity among the Indians.

John Adams, representing Massachusetts, and George Washington, representing Virginia, were present at these early congressional meetings. On March 16, 1776, "by order of Congress" a "day of Humiliation, Fasting and Prayer" where people of the nation were called on to "**acknowledge the over ruling providence of God**" and bewail their "**manifold sins and transgressions**, and, by a sincere repentance and amendment of life, appease his righteous displeasure, and, **through the merits and mediation of Jesus Christ**, obtain his pardon and forgiveness."[10]

Congress set aside December 18, 1777 as a day of thanksgiving so the American people "may express the grateful feelings of their hearts and consecrate themselves to the service of their divine benefactor"[11] and on which they might "join the penitent confession of their manifold sins… that it may please God, **through the merits of Jesus Christ**, mercifully to forgive and blot them out of remembrance." Congress also recommended that Americans petition God "to prosper the means of religion

---

10. Original document can be viewed at https://bit.ly/3mFdTTF

11. In another context, "divine benefactor" would be viewed as a deist ascription to an unnamed deity. It's obvious that in this context the Christian God is in view.

for the promotion and enlargement of that kingdom which consists in righteousness, **peace and joy in the Holy Ghost.**"[12] Keep in mind that these two proclamations precede (1774) and follow (1777) the drafting of the Declaration of Independence.

Professor Stone is correct that there were traditional Christians and deists among the Founders. "Around the time of the American Revolution," Robert Royal, president of the Faith and Reason Institute, writes that "a significant *minority* of the founders and the other colonists had been influenced by a moderate deism of the British sort that also retained strong elements of Christianity. Few, however, were deists properly speaking; most were out-and-out Christians."[13] The deists shaped their moral worldview from Christianity, picking and choosing what they liked and disliked and then constructed a hybrid religious model. Even Deism could not pass muster in today's government schools.

Anyway, I don't know how appealing to deists of any type helps Professor Stone's case. There are few card-carrying members of the ACLU who would accept the religious tenets and political applications of eighteenth-century deists or even Unitarians. Deists and Unitarians believed in a personal and transcendent God and appealed to Him frequently in political discourse.[14] If a candidate used deistic and Unitarian language in a

12. A copy of the original document can be viewed at https://bit.ly/3mF-dTTF. The proclamation can also be seen in Gary DeMar, *America's Christian History* (Powder Springs, GA: American Vision, 2005), 252.

13. Robert Royal, *The God That Did Not Fail: How Religion Built and Sustains the West* (New York: Encounter Books, 2006), 206. Emphasis added. For some helpful comments on the "unpopularity of deism" in the colonies, see Herbert M. Morais, *Deism in Eighteenth Century America* (New York: Russell & Russell, [1934] 1960), 91–98.

14. Alice M. Baldwin, *The New England Clergy and the American Revolution*

political speech today, the ACLU would be the first to proclaim that such attributions were a clear violation of the "constitutional doctrine" of the "separation of church and state."

I doubt that few Christians would disagree with Professor Stone's statement that the Founders "believed that a benevolent Supreme Being had created the universe and the laws of nature and had given man the power of reason with which to discover the meaning of those laws." I wonder if he would allow such a view to enter the discussion of human origins in a public-school classroom. If it was good enough for the Founders of our country, it certainly ought to be good enough for the young citizens of our country.

The rise of the New Atheists would nullify the claim that there is a "benevolent Supreme Being" who "had created the Universe." They would also reject the notion that a Supreme Being "had given man the power to reason." Professor Stone is doing what the deists did; he is borrowing from the Christian worldview to make his reason-alone worldview work. I suggest that he take time to study where an Enlightenment cut off from God will take us. It's not a pretty picture with heads falling into baskets, blood running in the streets, and approval coming from receptive "citizens."[15]

(New York: Frederick Ungar Publishing, [1928] 1958) and Franklin R. Cole, ed., *They Preached Liberty* (Indianapolis: LibertyPress, 1976).

15. Christopher Hitchens, *God is Not Great: How Religion Poisons Everything* (New York: Twelve Books, Hachette Book Group, 2007); Richard Dawkins, *The God Delusion* (Houghton Mifflin, 2006); Daniel C. Dennett, *Breaking the Spell: Religion as a Natural Phenomenon* (New York: Penguin, 2007); Sam Harris, *Letter to a Christian Nation* (New York: Knopf, 2006). For responses, see Douglas Wilson, *Letter from a Christian Citizen* (Powder Springs, GA: American Vision, 2007) and Joel McDurmon, *The Return of the Village Atheist* (Powder Springs, GA: American Vision, 2007).

NO CORNER ON IRRATIONALITY

Professor Stone argues that some of the Founders "viewed religious passion as irrational and dangerously divisive...and challenged, both publicly and privately, the dogmas of traditional Christianity." Some religious passion is irrational, but so is some political passion rooted in irreligion. And I dare say that some legal passion is irrational and dangerously divisive as well. Passion and division affect every major social issue of our day, from homosexual marriage to abortion rights and almost everything in between. The 1973 *Roe v. Wade* pro-abortion decision is viewed by many legal, moral, and political theorists as irrational and dangerously divisive.

PUTTING THE FOUNDERS TO THE TEST

Professor Stone centers his historical analysis on the views of Benjamin Franklin, Thomas Jefferson, John Adams, George Washington, and Thomas Paine, so that's where I'll concentrate my efforts. Keep in mind, however, that America's founding rests on more than the views and actions of these five men. Neither Franklin nor Jefferson had a hand in drafting the Constitution, and Paine was a British citizen.

BENJAMIN FRANKLIN

Benjamin Franklin went through a religious pilgrimage in his long life. There is little doubt that in his early years he was quite the religious skeptic but never an atheist. At the Pennsylvania Convention of 1776, "Franklin, who presided, was apparently

unable to stop the Convention from incorporating a constitutional provision stating that every representative was to declare
his belief in the divine inspiration of the Bible."[16] This shows
that there was a strong relationship between the Christian religion and civil government and that Franklin's views were a
minority position. He read the writings of English deists as a
young man, but "later experience and reflection caused him to
retreat somewhat from the thoroughgoing deism of his early
life.... Indeed Franklin's views on providence and prayer were
quite inconsistent with the deistic conception of an absentee
God who does not and who could not, in consistency with the
perfection of his work of creation and his impartial nature, interfere in the affairs of men."[17]

He states in his *Autobiography*, "I never doubted, for instance, the existence of the Deity; that he made the world, and
govern'd it by his Providence; that the most acceptable service
of God was the doing good to man; that our souls are immor-
tal; and that all crime will be punished, and virtue rewarded,
either here or hereafter."[18] Franklin became disenchanted with
much of what passed for Christianity in his day. He recalls waiting expectantly for comments from a minister who took as his
text, "Finally, brethren, whatever is true, whatever is honorable,
whatever is right, whatever is pure, whatever is lovely, whatever
is of good repute, if there is any excellence and if anything worthy of praise, dwell on these things" (Phil. 4:8). He comments,
"And I imagin'd, in a sermon on such a text, we could not miss

16. Morais, *Deism in Eighteenth Century America*, 91.

17. John Orr, *English Deism: Its Roots and Its Fruits* (Grand Rapids, MI: Eerdmans, 1935), 211.

18. Benjamin Franklin, *Autobiography*, ed. John Bigelow (Philadelphia: J. B. Lippincott, 1868), 211.

of having some morality." Instead of deriving moral application from the text, the minister went on to call for ceremonial and ecclesiastical works. Franklin went on to comment, "these might be all good things; but as they were not the kind of good things that I expected from that text, I despaired of ever meeting with them from any other, was disgusted, and attended his preaching no more."[19] Franklin's disappointment wasn't with the text, but an unfounded application of the text.

It was Franklin who addressed the Constitutional Convention by reminding those in attendance of "a superintending Providence" in their favor that brought them to their unique place that would make history.[20] He cited Psalm 127:1 to establish his point: "Unless the LORD builds the house, they labour in vain who build it." He went on to say something non-deistic, seeing "proofs" that "God rules in the affairs of men," and saying that without God's "concurring aid, we shall succeed in this political building no better than the builders of Babel" (Gen. 11:1– 9).[21]

It was Franklin and Jefferson who called for the phrase "Rebellion to Tyrants is Obedience to God" to be placed on the Great Seal of the United States (the phrase is the motto of the state of Virginia). In addition, Franklin wanted the following to adorn the front face of the seal:

> Moses standing on the Shore, and extending his Hand over the
> Sea, thereby causing the same to overwhelm Pharaoh who is

---

19. Franklin, *Autobiography*, 212–213.

20. See https://bit.ly/3mFdTTF

21. After the Convention Franklin's recommendation for an "officiate" (chaplain) was acted upon on April 9, 1789. Two chaplains were appointed, one to the House of Representatives and one to the Senate, with a salary of $500 each with no thought of violating the Constitution.

sitting in an open Chariot, a Crown on his Head and a Sword in his Hand. Rays from a Pillar of Fire in the Clouds reaching to Moses, to express that he acts by Command of the Deity.[22]

Franklin also declared, "Man will ultimately be governed by God or by tyrants."[23] I suspect that if some politician used similar religious terminology today, he would be denounced by the press as a "religious fundamentalist," dismissed as a "theocrat" and dangerous to the Republic by the ACLU and excoriated by Professor Stone for having a "disturbingly distorted version of history."

THOMAS JEFFERSON

Thomas Jefferson kept most of his religious views private, and his "separation of church and state" language was not used until 1802, nearly thirteen years after the drafting of the First Amendment. It's unfortunate that it has become substitute language for the actual wording of the First Amendment and distorted its meaning. In fact, in *ACLU of Kentucky, et al. v. Mercer County, Kentucky, et al.* (December 20, 2005), the United States Court of Appeals for the Sixth Circuit stated that while "the ACLU makes repeated reference to 'the separation of church and state,' [t]his extra-constitutional construct has grown tiresome." The court went on to argue the following:

> The First Amendment does not demand a wall of separation between church and state. *See Lynch*, 465 U.S. at 673; *Lemon*, 403 U.S. at 614; *Zorach v. Clauson*, 343 U.S. 306, 312 (1952); *Brown v. Gilmore*, 258 F.3d 265, 274 (4th Cir. 2001);

---

22. First Great Seal Committee (July/August 1776): https://bit.ly/3ckCybI
23. See Cole, *They Preached Liberty*, 5.

Stark v. Indep. Sch. Dist., No. 640., 123 F.3d 1068, 1076 (8th Cir. 1997); *see also Capitol Square*, 243 F.3d at 300 (dismissing strict separatism as "a notion that simply perverts our history"). Our Nation's history is replete with governmental acknowledgment and in some cases, accommodation of religion. *See, e.g., Marsh v. Chambers*, 463 U.S. 783 (1983) (upholding legislative prayer); *McGowan v. Maryland*, 366 U.S. 420 (1961) (upholding Sunday closing laws); *see also Lynch*, 465 U.S. at 674 ("There is an unbroken history of official acknowledgment by all three branches of government of the role of religion in American life from at least 1789."); *Capitol Square*, 243 F.3d at 293–99 (describing historical examples of governmental involvement with religion). After all, "[w]e are a religious people whose institutions presuppose a Supreme Being." *Zorach*, 343 U.S. at 313. Thus, state recognition of religion that falls short of endorsement is constitutionally permissible.[24]

Jefferson's views on Christianity were hardly credible for someone of his intellect and erudition. Like Professor Stone, Jefferson picked from the gospels what suited his rationalistic presuppositions.[25] Convenient, but hardly the work of a scholar. Nevertheless, for all of his anti-biblical statements and beliefs, Jefferson understood that "no system of morality would work for the common man or woman 'without the sanction of divine authority stampt upon it.'"[26]

---

24. *ACLU of Kentucky, et al. v. Mercer County, Kentucky, et al.* (December 20, 2005): https://bit.ly/3aX7NJ3

25. Thomas Jefferson, *The Life and Morals of Jesus Christ of Nazareth*. Various editions. Often published and recognized as *The Jefferson Bible*.

26. Edwin S. Gaustad, *Neither King Nor Prelate: Religion and the New Nation, 1776–1826*, rev. ed. (Grand Rapids, MI: Eerdmans, [1987] 1993), 105.

JOHN ADAMS

Professor Stone appeals next to John Adams who he identifies as a Unitarian. We find the following from Adams' *Diary* dated July 26, 1796:

> The Christian religion is, above all the Religions that ever pre-vailed or existed in ancient or modern Times, the Religion of Wisdom, Virtue, Equity, and humanity, let the Blackguard [Thomas] Paine say what he will; it is Resignation to God, it is Goodness itself to Man.[27]

Adams expressed his religious views on numerous occasions, but his call for a National Fast Day on March 6, 1799, is the most expressive. In it he described the Bible as "the Volume of Inspiration" and acknowledged "the growing providence of a Supreme Being and of the accountableness of men to Him as the searcher of hearts and righteous distributer of rewards and punishments." The Proclamation recommended the following:

> [That April 15, 1799 is to] be observed throughout the United States of America as a day of solemn humiliation, fasting, and prayer; that the citizens on that day abstain, as far as may be, from their secular occupation, and devote the time to the sa-cred duties of religion, in public and in private; that they call to mind our numerous offenses against the most high God, confess them before Him with the sincerest penitence, im-plore his pardoning mercy, through the Great Mediator and Redeemer, for our past transgressions, and that through the

---

27. John Adams, *The Diary and Autobiography of John Adams*, ed. L.H. But-terfield, 4 vols. (Cambridge, MA: The Belknap Press of Harvard University Press, 1962), 3:233–234.

grace of His Holy Spirit, we may be disposed and enabled to yield a more suitable obedience to his righteous requisitions in time to come; that He would interpose to arrest the progress of that impiety and licentiousness in principle and practice so offensive to Himself and so ruinous to mankind; that He would make us deeply sensible that "righteousness exalteth a nation, but sin is a reproach to any people [Proverbs 14:34]."[28]

Professor Stone reduces the religion of John Adams, based on a letter he had written to Jefferson, as "captured in the phrase, 'Be just and good.'" Jefferson had expressed a similar sentiment: "fear God and love thy neighbor."[29] A question remains: What determines what's just and good? Jefferson and Adams were living at a time when Christianity prevailed, and it was Jefferson who appealed to the gospels to make his case for his "wee little book" on morality based on the ethics of Jesus. But there were other letters that Adams had written to Jefferson on the subject of religion: "The general principles, on which the Fathers achieved independence, were... the general principles of Christianity"[30] and "Without religion this world would be something not fit to be mentioned in polite society, I mean hell."[31] Both men borrowed the moral capital of Christianity to make their case for a just society. Neither man was an atheist, and if asked

28. John Adams, "National Fast Day," Richardson, ed., *A Compilation of the Messages and Papers of the Presidents*, 1:284–286.

29. Quoted in Edwin S. Gaustad, *Sworn on the Altar of God: A Religious Biography of Thomas Jefferson* (Grand Rapids, MI: Eerdmans, 1996), 135.

30. John Adams to Thomas Jefferson (June 28, 1813) in Lester J. Cappon, ed., *The Adams-Jefferson Letters*, 2 vols. (Chapel Hill, NC: University of North Carolina Press, 1959), 2:339–340.

31. John Adams to Thomas Jefferson (April 19, 1817) in Thomas Jefferson, *The Writings of Thomas Jefferson* (Washington, DC: The Thomas Jefferson Memorial Association, 1904), 15:105.

to teach in today's public schools, they would be forbidden to state their religious beliefs.

GEORGE WASHINGTON

Next on Professor Stone's list of historical witnesses is George Washington. During the War for Independence, Washington wrote the following to Brig. General Thomas Nelson:

> The Hand of providence has been so conspicuous in all this, that he must be worse than an infidel that lacks faith, and more than wicked, that has not gratitude enough to acknowledge his obligations.[32]

As President, Washington stated that "it is the duty of all *nations* to acknowledge the providence of Almighty God, to obey His will, to be grateful for His benefits, and humbly to implore His protection and favor." In his Thanksgiving Proclamation of October 3, 1789, to write, that as a nation "we may then unite in most humbly offering our prayers and supplications to the great *Lord and Ruler of Nations*, and beseech Him to pardon our national and other transgressions."[33] Professor Stone's contrary evidence is at best hearsay. Washington's Thanksgiving Proclamation is direct evidence that he was no deist. When a person offers "prayers and supplication," he expects some sort of response. There is no response possible for the deist who believes God operates as an absentee landlord. In his Farewell address of 1796, Washington stated the following:

---

32. George Washington's letter of August 20, 1778 to Brig. General Thomas Nelson, in John C. Fitzpatrick, ed., *The Writings of George Washington* (Washington, D.C.: U.S. Government Printing Office, 1932), 12:343.

33. George Washington, "Proclamation: A National Thanksgiving," *A Compilation of the Messages and Papers of the Presidents, 1789–1902*, 1:64.

Of all the dispositions and habits which lead to political prosperity, **religion and morality are indispensable supports**. In vain would that man claim the tribute of patriotism, who should labor to subvert these great pillars of human happiness, these firmest props of the duties of men and citizens. The mere politician, equally with the pious man, ought to respect and to cherish them. A volume could not trace all their connections with private and public felicity. Let it simply be asked: **Where is the security for property, for reputation, for life, if the sense of religious obligation desert the oaths which are the instruments of investigation in courts of justice?** And let us with caution indulge the supposition that morality can be maintained without religion. Whatever may be conceded to the influence of refined education on minds of peculiar structure, **reason and experience both forbid us to expect that national morality can prevail in exclusion of religious principle.**[34]

Notice the connection of religion and morality and that religion and morality led to "political prosperity." While noting that there are "slight shades of difference," the people "have the same religion, manners, habits, and political principles." This "same religion" was Christianity. Even though not everyone in the early stages of our nation was a Christian, there was a spillover effect of biblical morality that most imbibed.

THOMAS PAINE

As usual, Tom Paine is called forth as a Founder of the American Republic. But is it the Paine of *Common Sense* or the Paine of *The*

---

34. George Washington, "Farewell Address" (1796): www.yale.edu/lawweb/avalon/washing.htm

Rights of Man (1791) and *The Age of Reason* (1793–1794)? Since *Common Sense* was written on the eve of the Revolution and *The Rights of Man* and *The Age of Reason* were written after the ratification of the Constitution, we should begin with *Common Sense*. Paine's *Common Sense* put forth arguments for independence from Great Britain. How did he argue his case? What were his sources?

A. J. Ayer remarks that "the first argument that Paine brings against the institution of kingship is scriptural."[35] Paine declared that

> government by kings was first introduced into the world by the Heathens, from which the children of Israel copied the custom.... As the exalting of one man so greatly above the rest cannot be justified on the equal rights of nature, so neither can it be defended on the authority of scripture; for the will of the Almighty, as declared by Gideon and the prophet Samuel, expressly disapproves of government by kings [Judges 8:22–23; 1 Sam. 8]. All anti-monarchical parts of scripture have been smoothly glossed over in monarchical governments, but they undoubtedly merit the attention of countries which have their governments yet to form. '*Render unto Caesar the things which are Caesar's*' is the scriptural doctrine of courts, yet it is no support of monarchical government, for the Jews at that time were without a king, and in a state of vassalage to the Romans.[36]

Paine has an extended discussion of Judges 8:22–23 where he describes "the King of Heaven" to be Israel's "proper sover-

---

35. A.J. Ayer, *Thomas Paine* (New York: Atheneum, 1988), 40. Ayer remarks that that his appeal to the Old Testament is curious "in view of the want of respect he was later to show for the Old Testament" (40).

36. Thomas Paine, *Common Sense* (New York: Barnes & Noble, [1776] 1995), 10. *Common Sense* can be accessed online at https://bit.ly/31shWKK

eign."[37] He then spends several pages quoting, discussing, and making application of the importance of 1 Samuel 8 to the modern situation. He concludes this section of *Common Sense* with these words: "In short, monarchy and succession have laid (not this or that kingdom only) by the world in blood and ashes. 'Tis a form of government which the word of God bears testimony against, and blood will attend it."[38]

It seems that Professor Stone trimmed this bit of history from Paine's body of work. Instead, he only quotes from his later publications which are anti-Christian but not atheistic. Consider his views of creation from his 1787 "Discourse at the Society of Theophilanthropists in Paris":

> It has been the error of schools to teach astronomy, and all the other sciences and subjects of natural philosophy, as accomplishments only; whereas they should be taught theologically, or with reference to the Being who is the Author of them: for all the principles of science are of divine origin. Man cannot make, or invent, or contrive principles; he can only discover them, and he ought to look through the discovery to the Author. When we examine an extraordinary piece of machinery, an astonishing pile of architecture, a well-executed statue, or a highly-finished painting where life and action are imitated, and habit only prevents our mistaking a surface of light and shade for cubical solidity, our ideas are naturally led to think of the extensive genius and talent of the artist. When we study the elements of geometry, we think of Euclid. When we speak of gravitation, we think of Newton. How, then, is it that when we study the works of

---

37. Paine, *Common Sense*, 11.
38. Paine, *Common Sense*, 11–14.

God in creation, we stop short and do not think of God? It is from the error of the schools in having taught those subjects as accomplishments only and thereby separated the study of them from the Being who is the Author of them....The evil that has resulted from the error of the schools in teaching natural philosophy as an accomplishment only has been that of generating in the pupils a species of atheism. Instead of looking through the works of creation to the Creator Himself, they stop short and employ the knowledge they acquire to create doubts of His existence. They labor with studied ingenuity to ascribe everything they behold to innate properties of matter and jump over all the rest by saying that matter is eternal. And when we speak of looking through nature up to nature's God, we speak philosophically the same rational language as when we speak of looking through human laws up to the power that ordained them. God is the power of first cause, nature is the law, and matter is the subject acted upon. But infidelity, by ascribing every phenomenon to properties of matter, conceives a system for which it cannot account and yet it pretends to demonstrate.[39]

Could the above comments by Paine be worked into the curriculum of today's public schools? I doubt it.

How much support did Paine get from the Founders in his later works where he repudiated the Bible and Christianity but still remained a theist? We've already read that Adams called him a "blackguard." Samuel Adams wrote Paine a stiff rebuke,

---

39. Thomas Paine, *Life and Writings of Thomas Paine*, ed. Daniel Edwin Wheeler, 10 vols. (New York: Printed by Vincent Parke and Company, 1908), 7:2–8, "The Existence of God," A Discourse at the Society of Theophilanthropists, Paris. Also see Thomas Paine, "Discourse Delivered to the Society of Theophilanthropists at Paris" in *The Theological Works of Thomas Paine* (London: R. Carlile, 1818), 4–5.

telling him, "[W]hen I heard you had turned your mind to a defence of infidelity, I felt myself much astonished and more grieved that you had attempted a measure so injurious to the feelings and so repugnant to the true interest of so great a part of the citizens of the United States."[40] In his Introduction to *Common Sense*, Gregory Tietjen writes that Paine's "explicit expressions of disbelief roused the faithful to fury and earned Paine an enmity that destroyed the good reputation he enjoyed for his earlier activities in behalf of the American cause.... [H]is polemics against President Washington had lost him the loyalty of many patriots, and his religious beliefs had earned him the wrath of the Christian faithful."[41] Even the usually tolerant Quakers refused him burial in a Quaker graveyard.

Professor Stone describes the views of the later Paine as "shockingly blunt and 'politically incorrect' to modern ears, but they were in fact the views of many of our most revered Founders. The fable that the United States was founded as a Christian Nation is just that—a fable." Paine's *Common Sense*, with its biblical arguments from the Old and New Testaments, is direct testimony that Stone is wrong. Mark A. Noll, professor of history at the University of Notre Dame, argues, "If Paine's *Age of Reason* (with its dismissive attitude toward the Old Testament) had been published before *Common Sense* (with its full deployment of Scripture in support of republican freedom), the quarrel with Britain may have taken a different course. It is also likely that the allegiance of traditional Christian believers to republican liberty might not

---

40. William V. Wells, *The Life and Public Services of Samuel Adams* (Boston: Little, Brown and Co., 1865), 3:372–373. Letter to Thomas Paine on November 30, 1802.

41. Gregory Tietjen, "Introduction," in Paine, *Common Sense*, xii.

have been so thoroughly cemented. And it is possible that the intimate relation between republican reasoning and trust in traditional Scripture, which became so important after the turn of the new century, would not have occurred as it did."[42] Robert Royal comments that "for Paine—a skillful polemicist whose attachment to Christianity was always uncertain and seems eventually to have evaporated—to use an argument such as this at a delicate moment testifies, at the very least, to the power of religious arguments for liberty in America."[43] John Orr remarks that Paine received a "cold reception...when he returned from France after publishing his deistic book *The Age of Reason*." This reaction "does not suggest that deism was as popular in America as some" historical accounts "might lead one to suppose."[44]

THE DECLARATION OF INDEPENDENCE

Professor Stone's objection that the Declaration of Independence is a deist document does not fit the definition when it uses phrases like the "Supreme Judge of the World for the Rectitude of our Intentions" and "a firm reliance on the Protection of divine Providence." A deistic God does not judge or protect. He's indifferent to the world He created. There is a further problem with the phrase that asserts that rights are an endowment from the "Creator." How would this statement go over in Public Schools where evolution without any hint of a Creator is taught? Could the Declaration of Independence pass legal scrutiny to-

---

42. Mark A. Noll, *America's God: From Jonathan Edwards to Abraham Lincoln* (New York: Oxford University Press, 2002), 84.
43. Royal, *The God that Did Not Fail*, 216.
44. Orr, *English Desim*, 219.

day? I doubt it. While Professor Stone asserts that the Declaration is not an Evangelical document, it seems quite odd that so many of the 56 men who signed it were members of Evangelical churches, one of whom was Presbyterian clergyman John Witherspoon. Had they acquiesced to deism? I doubt it. The terms used were in common usage by orthodox Christian believers.[45]

"IN THE YEAR OF OUR LORD"

Next we come to the Constitution, a governing document created by the states for a limited purpose. Professor Stone states that the Constitution does not "invoke the deity at all." As we've seen, there were numerous official government documents that are specific in their mention of God, Jesus Christ, and the Holy Spirit. All the state constitutions invoked "the deity." But Professor Stone makes no mention of these. In Article 1, section 7 of the Constitution, Sunday is set aside as a day of rest for the President. Just above George Washington's signature the following phrase appears: "Done in the Year of our Lord...one thousand seven hundred and Eighty-seven." These examples might seem inconsequential, but keep in mind that people like Professor Stone argue that the constitutional framers wanted to separate religion from every facet of government. Here was a perfect opportunity to do it. The French revolutionaries abolished the seven-day biblical week and instituted a ten-day week. Their revolutionary calendar began with a new "Year One." Those who fomented the revolution made every effort to distance themselves from Christianity. Our framers did not.

---

45. See Gary Amos, *Defending the Declaration* (Brentwood, TN: Wolgemuth and Hyatt, 1989).

PRIVATELY HELD BUT
POLITICALLY FORBIDDEN

Professor Stone admits that "the Founders were not anti-religion. They understood that religion could help nurture the public morality necessary to a self-governing society," but only privately and personally. What does this mean? If a person holds private and personal religious beliefs, does this preclude him from applying them in the area of public policy? That's what Professor Stone believes. They "had no place in the political life of a nation dedicated to the separation of church and state." Our Founders didn't argue this way. Jefferson believed that no system of morality would work for the common man or woman "without the sanction of divine authority stampt upon it." Adams was equally adamant that "the general principles, on which the Fathers achieved independence, were…the general principles of Christianity." Should someone who held opinions against slavery based on religious principles have kept them private? There would have been no civil rights movement or resistance to Adolf Hitler if the privately held but politically forbidden paradigm had been followed as Professor Stone suggests. Professor Stone's narrowly focused views would be destructive to our Republic. In fact, we are seeing the destruction as we debate this issue.

MISREADING THE FIRST AMENDMENT

As usual, there is the obligatory genuflection to the "separation of church and state." Who is arguing for combining them? The First Amendment is not dealing with church-state issues. The prohibition is directed against Congress and what it can't do.

The states with their religious state constitutions insisted on an amendment protecting them from a strong national government, including the topic of religion. The amendment prohibits Congress from establishing a religion or prohibiting the free exercise thereof.

I don't see how a manger scene, the mention of Christmas, singing Christmas carols, a valedictorian address invoking God,[46] praying at a government meeting for wisdom and direction, or any number of religious ceremonies is a violation of the First Amendment as originally conceived. There is no call to force anyone to believe anything, go to church, or pay a tithe. But like our founders, we need to recognize that the State is not the grantor of rights or freedoms. They are an endowment from our Creator, and it is the duty of civil governments to ensure that these rights and freedoms remain. The logic is simple: No God, no rights. What the State gives, the State can take away.

Professor Stone writes that our founders "would have been appalled at the idea of the federal government sponsoring 'faith-based' initiatives." Well, I'm appalled that money is taken from me and used to support a government education system that teaches a religious worldview contrary to what I believe. Talk about a "faith-based" initiative.

I am quite happy to tolerate Professor Stone's secularism "as long as he keeps it out of our government."

THE TREATY OF TRIPOLI OF 1797

Professor Stone brings up the 1797 "Treaty of Tripoli" that includes the phrase from Article 11 that "the Government of the

---

46. www.rutherford.org/KeyCases/McComb.asp

United States...is not in any sense founded on the Christian religion."[47] Adams signed it, and so did a unanimous Congress, most of whom were orthodox Christians.[48] How can this be explained in terms of the historical record? Forrest Church offers this bit of commentary on Article 11:

> Too much can be made of this document as a proof text that Adams believed, as the treaty says, that "the United States is by no means founded on the Christian religion." Washington, Jefferson, and Madison certainly could have endorsed this clause, but Adams, at this point in his political career, anyway, could not. In signing the treaty, he either glossed over the eleventh article as being of no moment or read its meaning narrowly. At the time Adams expressly believed that the U.S. government could not prosper apart from a sound Christian foundation.[49]

The statement in the 1797 treaty was nothing more than a pronouncement "that 'the Christian religion' as a formal institution was not a part of the American government in the same way that the religious structures of Islam are a part of Islamic governments."[50] The statement was to assure a Muslim government that America would not depose a Muslim government and impose Christianity by force, something Islamic governments do when they conquer a people.

---

47. William M. Malloy, *Treaties, Conventions, International Acts, Protocols and Agreements between the United States of America and Other Powers, 1776–1909*, 4 vols. (New York: Greenwood Press, [1910] 1968), 2:1786.

48. For a more complete study of the Treaty with Tripoli, see Gary DeMar, *America's 200-Year War with Terror: The Strange Case of the Treaty of Tripoli* (Powder Springs, GA: American Vision, 2009).

49. Forrest Church, *So Help Me God: The Founding Fathers and the First Great Battle Over Church and State* (Orlando: Harcourt, Inc., 2007), 208.

50. Amos, *Defending the Declaration*, 9.

According to Frank Lambert, Professor of History at Purdue University, the assurances found in Article 11 were "intended to allay the fears of the Muslim state by insisting that religion would not govern how the treaty was interpreted and enforced. John Adams and the Senate made clear that the pact was between two sovereign states, not between two religious powers."[51] This is an important point missed by some atheists and historical revisionists (on purpose?).

Islam merged mosque and State. In the United States, there is a jurisdictional separation between church and State. The First Amendment forbids Congress from interfering in the religious affairs of the states most of which were particularly Christian in their constitutions.

Even the late anti-theist Christopher Hitchens got it right: "secularists like myself who like to cite this treaty must concede that its conciliatory language was part of America's attempt to come to terms with Barbary demands."[52]

The Barbary pirates habitually preyed on ships from "Christian nations," enslaving "Christian" seamen. Since this was a treaty between the United States and an Islamic government, was America not one of these Christian nations? "Barbary was Christendom's Gulag Archipelago."[53] Joseph Wheelan's historical assessment of the time is on target. "Except for its Native American population and a small percentage of Jews, the United States was solidly Christian, while the North African

---

51. Quoted in Sam Magnussen, "History Was Quoted Out of Context," *The Reflector* (March 13, 2013).

52. Christopher Hitchens, "Jefferson Versus the Muslim Pirates," *City Journal* (April 20, 2007).

53. Stephen Clissold, *The Barbary Slaves* (New York: Barnes & Noble, [1977] 1992), 4.

regencies were just as solidly Muslim—openly hostile toward Christians."[54]

In drafting the treaty, the United States was assuring the Dey (ruler) of Tripoli that in its struggle with the pirates "it has in itself no character of enmity against the laws, religion or tranquility of Musselmen"(an archaic or foreign-language term for Muslims), that "the said states never have entered into any war or act of hostility against any Mehomitan [Muslim] nation" due to religious considerations.[55] These are the qualifying statements in the treaty that explain why the phrase "founded on the Christian religion" was used. It had nothing to do with the religious character of the individual states that made up the national government.

The Dey of Tripoli had to be convinced that America, as a Christian nation based on the reading of the state constitutions and official documents going back nearly two hundred years, would not impose its religion on the Muslim people. "Could it have been that in Article 11, America was assuring Tripoli and all of the Barbary States that the United States did not have a state church system and would therefore not attack Tripoli for religious reasons of forced conversion?"[56] This seems to be the best explanation of the phrase found in Article 11 of the 1797 Treaty.[57]

The eleventh article of the English version of the treaty "has no equivalent whatever in the Arabic."[58] In addition, there are

54. Joseph Wheelan, *Jefferson's War: America's First War on Terror, 1801–1805* (New York: Carroll & Graf Publishers, 2003), 7.

55. Malloy, *Treaties, etc.*, 2:1786.

56. John W. Whitehead, "The Treaty of Tripoli," *The Rutherford Institute* (January/February 1985), 11.

57. Also see David Aikman, *The Delusion of Disbelief* (Carol Stream, IL: Tyndale, 2008), 157–162.

58. Snouck Hurgronje, "The Barbary Treaties: The Annotated Translation of 1930": https://bit.ly/3hVrLH7

descriptions of "American Christians," "Christian enemies," "Christians with whom we are at peace," and "like all the other Christian nations" in the "Annotated Translation of 1930."[59] Presumably this means that Tripoli considered the United States to be a Christian nation as well as other nations at the time.

Not everyone was happy with the conciliatory language of the treaty. Secretary of War James McHenry, under John Adams, spoke out openly about the language of the Treaty of Tripoli. He wrote the following to the Secretary of the Treasury Oliver Wolcott, Jr. on September 26, 1800:

> The Senate, my good friend, and I said so at the time, ought never to have ratified the treaty alluded to, with the declaration that "the government of the United States, is not, in any sense, founded on the Christian religion." What else is it founded on? This act always appeared to me like *trampling upon the cross.* I do not recollect that Barlow was even reprimanded for this outrage upon the government and religion.[60]

John Adams, in a letter to Thomas Jefferson dated June 28, 1813, stated the following regarding Christianity:

> The general principles on which the fathers achieved independence, were the only principles in which that beautiful assembly of young men could unite, and these principles only could be intended by them in their address, or by me in my answer. And what were these general principles? I answer, the general principles of Christianity, in which all those sects were united,

---

59. https://bit.ly/3hVrLH7

60. "Letter from James McHenry to John Adams," in *Memoirs of the Administrations of Washington and John Adams: Edited from the Papers of Oliver Wolcott, Secretary of the Treasury,* 2 vols. (New York: William Van Norden, 1846), 2:421.

and the general principles of English and American liberty, in which all those young men united, and which had united all parties in America, in majorities sufficient to assert and maintain her independence. Now I will avow, that I then believed and now believe that those general principles of Christianity are as eternal and immutable as the existence and attributes of God; and that those principles of liberty are as unalterable as human nature and our terrestrial, mundane system.

Adams also included the "general principles of English and American liberty," that also were based on the general principles of Christianity which can be seen in early colonial documents (e.g., The Mayflower Compact) and colonial charters and constitutions.[61]

Then there is the 1780 Massachusetts Constitution, the world's oldest functioning written constitution, which served as the model for the United States Constitution in 1787. Samuel W. Calhoun writes in his response to a Geoffrey Stone article.[62]

Adams was the principal draftsman [of the Massachusetts Constitution]…, a document that David McCullough calls "one of the most admirable, long-lasting achievements of …Adams's life."[63] The Preamble referred "to the constitution as 'a covenant' or 'compact' between the people and God."[64]

---

61. See Francis Newton Thorpe, *The Federal and State Constitutions, Colonial Charters, and Other Organic Laws of the States, Territories, and Colonies Now or Heretofore Forming the United States of America*, 7 vols. (Washington, D.C.: Government Printing Office, 1909).

62. Samuel W. Calhoun, "Getting the Framers Wrong: A Response to Professor Geoffrey Stone," *UCLA Law Review* (October 24, 2009): https://bit.ly/2YPV70K

63. David McCullough, *John Adams* (New York: Simon and Schuster 2001), 220.

64. John Witte, Jr., "A Most Mild and Equitable Establishment of Religion":

The language bespoke a "covenant ceremonial liturgy, rooted in the Hebrew Bible and in a New England tradition going back to the Mayflower Compact of 1620."[65] The Declaration of Rights, which followed the Preamble, "affirmed the 'duty' of all people to worship 'The Supreme Being, the great creator and preserver of the universe.'"[66] The Constitution also required that both the Governor and Lieutenant Governor "be of the Christian religion."[67] Even more significantly, the Constitution, in language not drafted by Adams but supported by him,[68] also stipulated "the payment of religious taxes in support of congregational ministers."[69]

These and many more indicators demonstrate that the enlightenment era did not erase America's Christian heritage.

John Adams and the Massachusetts Experiment" in James H. Hutson, ed., *Religion and the New Republic: Faith in the Founding of America* (Lanham, MD: Roman & Littlefield Publishers, 2000), 137–138 *supra* note 19, at 1, 19.

65. Witte, *"A Most Mild and Equitable Establishment of Religion,"* 137–138.

66. McCullough, *John Adams*, 221–22, note 56. The constitutional convention altered this language to make worshiping God "a right of all men, as well as a duty" (224).

67. Witte, *"A Most Mild and Equitable Establishment of Religion*, note 57, 10. "Article I. Any person chosen governor, lieutenant-governor, councillor, senator, or representative, and accepting the trust, shall, before he proceed to execute the duties of his place or office, make and subscribe the following declaration, viz:

"I, A.B., do declare that I believe the Christian religion, and have a firm persuasion of its truth; and that I am seized and possessed, in my own right, of the property required by the constitution, as one qualification for the office or place to which I am elected."

68. Witte, *"A Most Mild and Equitable Establishment of Religion*, 10–11, 24.

69. Witte, *"A Most Mild and Equitable Establishment of Religion*, 10. It is curious that McCullough does not mention this provision in discussing "notable changes" to Adams's draft made by the convention. See McCullough, *John Adams*, 224–25, note 56.

THE TREATY OF TRIPOLI OF 1805

It is important to note that the 1805 treaty with Tripoli, drafted during Jefferson's administration, differs from the 1797 Treaty in that the phrase "as the Government of the United States of America is not in any sense founded on the Christian Religion" is conspicuously absent. The following is from Article 14 of the 1805 treaty:

> As the Government of the United States of America, has in itself no character of enmity against the Laws, Religion or Tranquility of Musselmen, and as the said States never have entered into any voluntary war or act of hostility against any Mahometan Nation, except in the defence of their just rights to freely navigate the High Seas: It is declared by the contracting parties that no pretext arising from Religious Opinions, shall ever produce an interruption of the Harmony existing between the two Nations; . . . .

Once again, the issue of American interference in the internal affairs of an Islamic nation was the same issue that was stated in the 1797 treaty that made it necesssary. Assurances are still offered that the United States will not interfere with Tripoli's religion or laws. It's obvious that by 1805 the United States had greater bargaining power and did not have to knuckle under to the demands of this Muslim stronghold.[70] A strong navy and a contingent of Marines also helped but did not settle the issue as subsequent history shows.

---

70. Michael Beschloss mentions the fact that "a treaty favorable to the United States was signed in 1805," but says nothing about the 1797 treaty with its accommodationist language (*American Heritage Illustrated History of the Presidents* [New York: Times Books, 2000], 58).

"THE MOST HOLY AND UNDIVIDED TRINITY"

If treaties are going to be used to establish the religious foundation of America, then it's essential that we look at more than one treaty. In 1783, at the close of the war with Great Britain, a peace treaty was ratified that began with these words: "In the name of the Most Holy and Undivided Trinity. It having pleased the Divine Providence to dispose the hearts of the most serene and most potent Prince George the Third, by the Grace of God King of Great Britain."[71] The treaty was signed by John Adams, Benjamin Franklin, and John Jay. Keep in mind that it was Adams who signed the 1797 Treaty of Tripoli.

In 1822, the United States, along with Great Britain and Ireland, ratified a "Convention for Indemnity Under Award of Emperor of Russia as to the True Construction of the First Article of the Treaty of December 24, 1814."[72] It begins with the same words found in the Preamble to the 1783 treaty: "In the name of the Most Holy and Indivisible Trinity." Only Christianity teaches a Trinitarian view of God. There doesn't seem to have been any reluctance on the part of the American signers to affix their names to it.

The 1848 Treaty of Peace, Friendship, Limits and Settlement between the United States of America and the Mexican Republic, the peace treaty between the United States and Mexico that ended the Mexican–American War (1846–1848), begins with "In the name of Almighty God." The treaty also states that both countries are "under the protection of Almighty God, the author of peace...."[73]

71. Malloy, *Treaties, etc.*, 1:586.
72. Malloy, *Treaties, etc.*, 1:634.
73. Malloy, *Treaties, etc.*, 1:1107.

A CRITIC RESPONDS

Chris Rodda spends 35 pages on the "Treaties with the Barbary States" in her book *Liars for Jesus: The Religious Right's Alternative Version of American History* but never explains the context of the phrase. Furthermore, Rodda states that "the President, the Senate, and the people of the United States apparently accepted without question an official statement that '*the government of the United States of America is not in any sense founded on the Christian religion....*'" There surely were many Christians in the Senate. Why didn't they object to the statement?

Given the religious nature of all state constitutions, some of which were explicitly Christian (e.g., North Carolina), it seems rather odd that there were no protestations unless the statement had the particular purpose of assuring a Muslim stronghold that America did not merge Church and State. The language was designed to give assurances to Tripoli that the United States would not interfere in any way with "the law, *religion* or tranquility of Musselmen."

Rodda writes "that the Muslims in the Barbary states wrongly assumed that the United States was a Christian nation like the nations of Europe."[74] This is factually incorrect. The language of the official documents of the United States—state constitutions, the use of "the Year of our Lord" in the Federal Constitution, and calls for national days of prayer and thanksgiving with references to Jesus Christ were primary evidence that America was foundationally Christian but not officially Christian. How could these Islamic states thing otherwise? America did not have a State church. This all explains very well why the state-

---

74. Chris Rodda, *Liars for Jesus: The Religious Right's Alternate Version of American History*, vol. 1 (New Jersey: published by the author, 2006), 301.

ment regarding the "Christian religion" was added with only a few protestations (e.g., James McHenry).

Rodda offers this "explanation" as to why the "Christian religion" statement does not appear in the 1805 Treaty: "the events that occurred between 1797 and 1805 made it necessary to rewrite it."[75] But why? She states that "Tobias Lear left out the phrase '*is not in any sense founded on the Christian religion*'" but claims "there is nothing significant about this." How does she know this? If the phrase was significant for Rodda and her fellow skeptics when it appeared in the 1797 Treaty, it seems that leaving it out of the 1805 Treaty had some significance other than that the phrase "was unnecessary, and, with what was being added, made the sentence too long."[76]

CONCLUSION

Samuel W. Calhoun offers a helpful analysis of Professor Stone's inconsistencies by using his own words against him:

> Professor Stone concedes that virtually all the Founders, traditional religionists and otherwise, believed that religion was valuable in fostering "civic virtue," keeping alive "the best sense of moral obligation," and confining persons "within the bounds of social duty." It is completely unrealistic to think that a religious person's sense of right and wrong could ever be completely cabined within the private sphere....[77]

Amen!

75. Rodda, *Liars for Jesus,* 315.
76. Rodda, *Liars for Jesus,* 315.
77. Calhoun, "Getting the Framers Wrong."

Politics is Messy and the Lesser of Two Evils Conundrum

Two people are running for a political office. You have inside knowledge of what these candidates will do in the future. The first candidate will expand the military, implement confiscatory taxes, and enrich some of his trusted political allies with property stolen from the people.

The second candidate will commit adultery, be an accomplice to murder, be identified as a man of bloodshed, and sleep with a young woman, and his son will be his successor and increase the military beyond its constitutional limits and align himself with foreign powers by adopting their pagan religious practices.

These are your only two viable choices.

If you are at all familiar with the Bible, you know that the two candidates are King Saul and King David, and David's successor, Solomon. If you had this future knowledge, who would you choose? Would you say that you could not choose the "lesser of two evils" and thereby not vote for either one of them? But one of them (David) is God's choice to be king. What a dilemma.

Politics was as messy in biblical times as it is today. Biblical heroes like Gideon, Jephthah, Samuel, Barak, and Samson had their moral failings, and yet they are in the biblical "Hall of Faith":

> And what more shall I say? For time will fail me if I tell of Gideon [idolater], Barak [coward], Samson [womanizer], Jephthah [made a rash vow], of David [adulterer, accomplice to murder, man of bloodshed] and Samuel [a terrible father who raised two evil sons] and the prophets, **who by faith conquered kingdoms, performed acts of righteousness,** obtained promises, shut the mouths of lions, quenched the power of fire, escaped the edge of the sword, from weakness were made strong, became mighty in war, put foreign armies to flight (Heb. 11:32–34).

These were some very flawed people, and yet they are described as having "performed acts of righteousness." But there was a lot of unrighteousness mixed in. Samson was a very carnal man, and yet God used him. He was chosen by God to save Israel from the Philistines, and yet he demanded of his father and mother that they help him marry a pagan Philistine woman:

> Then Samson went down to Timnah and saw a woman in Timnah, one of the daughters of the Philistines. So he came back and told his father and mother, "I saw a woman in Timnah, one of the daughters of the Philistines; now therefore, get her for me as a wife." Then his father and his mother said to him, "Is there no woman among the daughters of your rela-

tives, or among all our people, that you go to take a wife from the uncircumcised Philistines?" But Samson said to his father, "Get her for me, for she looks good to me" (Judges 14:1–4).

We always need to keep in mind that "God has chosen the foolish things of the world to shame the wise, and God has chosen the weak things of the world to shame the things which are strong, and the base things of the world and the despised God has chosen, so that no man may boast before God" (1 Cor. 1:27–28). There is no perfection in this world. In most cases, we have to settle for the less than righteous while always pursuing righteousness. There aren't many Josephs or Daniels around. There was only one of each in the Bible.

None of this is to say that we should dismiss the sins of people running for public office. Far from it. Christians should strive to elect people who exemplify a righteous life. The fact is, however, we're not always given the opportunity to vote for such candidates.

The New Testament is equally messy. Jesus tells the Pharisees, "render to Caesar the things that are Caesar's; and to God the things that are God's" (Matt. 22:21)? Wasn't Caesar a pagan? Isn't everything God's? How do we know what things are Caesar's? It's obvious by Jesus' statement that not everything is Caesar's. Consider that Christians were called on to "submit . . . for the Lord's sake to every human institution, whether to a king as the one in authority, or to governors as sent by him for the punishment of evildoers and the praise of those who do right" (1 Pet. 2:13–14). Of course, there are exceptions (see chap. 7).

By the way, we don't live under Caesar in the strictest sense. Our system of civil government is decentralized with multiple jurisdictions and open to change. In the United States, rulers are bound by the limits of written constitutions at the state and national levels. This was not true in Rome, and yet God's people were to render to Caesar what was his.

The Jews living under Roman rule could not participate in politics. The Apostle Paul had dual citizenship which gave him some rights as a Roman citizen. He reproached the Roman rulers for his beatings and his jailing and called for a public apology for their actions(Acts 16:11–40) and later appealed to Caesar for relief from persecution (21:27–40).

Not all Roman citizens could vote. The Caesars were not elected to office by the people. Rome had its pantheon of gods, and in time the Caesars often included themselves among them. "By the time of Domitian (AD 81–96), it had become common to address him as *Dominus et Deus*, 'my Lord and God.'"[1]

Local rulers were chosen by Moses from among the people (Ex. 18:17–27). These appointed, not elected, under-governors were bound by a selective body of laws. Any dispute these men could not resolve was to be taken to Moses and ultimately to God. This is not our system. It's a system that is no longer available or attainable. We would need a Moses-like ruler who would appoint local governors and who also spoke directly to God. There wouldn't be any elections since there was no political competition in Israel.

There were elections of some sort in ancient Israel during the monarchy. The choice of Saul as king was a popular election (1 Sam. 8). "All Israel had come to Shechem to make Rehoboam king" (1 Kings 12:1). There was no competing ethical

---

1. Herbert Schlossberg, *Idols for Destruction: Christian Faith and its Confrontation with American Society* (Nashville, TN: Thomas Nelson, 1983), 185.

system like we have today. Jethro's advice to Moses was to teach the people "the statutes and the laws and make known to them the way in which they are to walk and the work they are to do" (18:20). This is great advice. Our nation's problem is that most people have no regard for a fixed set of revealed moral standards governing personal, social, or political affairs. This is true of much of the church.

The law in Israel was imposed on the people. There was no discussion or vote as to what the law would be. We live under a different political system with competing moral standards. As much as we might want a certain kind of candidate, there are competing special interest groups that also want a particular type of candidate to do their bidding. Until Christians start thinking and acting in terms of biblical values, we are stuck with a form of moral and political pluralism.

Our nation's political leadership reflects the moral pluralism of the people. For this to change, so we can get the type of leaders described by Jethro (Ex. 18:21), the people must change. We are not anywhere near this objective. That's why we had Hillary Clinton and Donald Trump running for President of the United States in 2016 and Trump and former Vice-President Joe Biden in 2020. Yes, I know, there are third-party candidates, but they don't have a chance even if all Christians who truly hold to biblical moral values voted for one of them. It's the nature of our political system.

Consider that Hillary Clinton has said, "The Bible was and remains the biggest influence on my thinking."[2] That's not possible when issues like abortion, same-sex sexuality, and socialis-

2. "Hillary Rodham Clinton: By the Book," *The New York Times* (June 11, 2014): https://nyti.ms/2G0SLGA

tic economic policies are considered. There is a general disconnect with many Christians on the relationship between biblical ethics and politics. Too many Christians believe that what they believe personally has no bearing on the political sphere. It was one of the reasons that often Christians opposed slavery personally but did not oppose it politically. They believed there were two standards—one for the Church and one for the State.

The early church made the best of a similar situation. The Apostle Paul had to appeal to the Roman government when he learned of a conspiracy by his fellow countrymen to kill him:

> When it was day, the Jews formed a conspiracy and bound themselves under an oath, saying that they would neither eat nor drink until they had killed Paul. There were more than forty who formed this plot. They came to the chief priests and the elders and said, "We have bound ourselves under a solemn oath to taste nothing until we have killed Paul" (Acts 23:12–14, 21).

To avoid being murdered by his countrymen (see Acts 9:23; 13:45, 50; 14:5; 17:5, 13; 18:12; 20:3, 19; 21:27; 2 Cor. 11:26; 1 Thess. 2:15), Paul appealed to Caesar (Acts 25:3, 11, 21, 25). There were no acknowledged civil law courts where Christians could adjudicate a case. Paul sought political protection from a pagan power rather than entrust himself to the Jewish court system whose members were obligated to follow God's law. But in his case and with Jesus they chose to discard the law in favor of their traditions (Mark 7:1–13) and to protect their positions of power. They believed they were doing the will of God, something Paul himself thought he was doing when he opposed Christians and oversaw the murder of Stephen (Acts 7:58).

What should we make of Paul's appeal to Caesar when he had written that the secular courts were governed by "the unrighteous" (1 Cor. 6:1)? The issues Paul was addressing among the Corinthians were most likely local and personal disagreements that could be handled by church elders and experts in God's law. Capital offenses and political disputes could not be tried by these courts.

Even though the Jews were under the heel of Rome, there was never a call for armed revolt. Jesus told Peter to put away his sword (John 18:10–11) and admonished Pilate that while He had at His "disposal more than twelve legions of angels," His kingdom does not advance by such methods (Matt. 26:53). This is an early indication that the Roman Empire would be conquered, not by armies, but by the proclamation of the gospel and the application of God's Word to every area of life. It's the gospel plus people who follow God's moral law in every area of life "including civil government and its limitations" that bring about change.

Christians cannot shrink from the scene when political decisions are hard to make. We need to be "wise as serpents and innocent as doves" (Matt. 10:16) while recognizing that "the sons of this age are often more shrewd in relation to their own kind than the sons of light" (Luke 16:8).

We live in a sinful world. There's no getting around this truth this side of heaven. No politician is perfect, as the Bible makes clear. We're always going to elect the lesser of two evils. I asked one Christian the following question: "Of the 535 members of Congress, who could you vote for?" He said, "none of them." Is this what we're left with? Until either a Joseph or a Daniel runs for office, Christians can't vote for anyone? Is this the lesson the Bible is teaching? I don't believe it is.

The first place to start to change the political landscape so that it conforms to biblical principles of leadership is to understand that civil government is only one government among many and is designed to be a limited government of specific enumerated powers at that. Our Constitution, a marvel of brevity, says as much in the Tenth Amendment.

> The powers not delegated to the United States by the Constitution, nor prohibited by it to the States, are reserved to the States respectively, or to the people.

Self-government under God is the starting point in the transformation of the political sphere. A person who can't govern himself well (not perfectly) can't govern well when other imperfect people are part of the mix.

To repeat what has been discussed in earlier chapters of this book, governing principles must be taught by word and example. Training in good government begins with family government. The Preface to *Elements of Civil Government* states, "This text-book begins 'at home.' The starting point is the family, the first form of government with which the child comes in contact."[3] Noah Webster's 1828 *Dictionary of the English Language* includes the following definition under the entry "government": "The exercise of authority by a parent or householder. 'Children are often ruined by a neglect of government in parents. Let family government be like that of our heavenly Father, mild, gentle and affectionate.'"

The church is a government. There are specific qualifications for church governors (elders) outlined by the Apostle Paul

---

3. Alex L. Peterman, *Elements of Civil Government: A Text-Book for Use in Public Schools, High Schools, and Normal Schools* (New York: American Book Company, [1891] 1903), 5.

(1 Tim. 3:2–7). Keep in mind that these are qualifications for Christians in an ecclesiastical setting that are transferable to the civil sphere. But not all candidates are going to exemplify these character traits. In most cases, however, the majority of people do want their civil servants to embody the qualities that Paul lists. Christians should strive to nurture and support such candidates.

We need to remember, however, that not every person's past is squeaky clean. Paul was an accomplice to murder (Acts 7:58), and he reminds the church of Corinth that "such were some of you" in the sins he lists (1 Cor. 6:11; also 12:2; Eph. 2:1–3; Titus 3:3–7).

Today, "government" has become the sole domain of the State, the civil sphere. When the State enlarges its jurisdictional boundaries without any regard to limits, it gradually assumes what God alone possesses: unlimited power and authority. Civil governments at all jurisdictional levels were designed by God to promote justice, not to be a dispenser of sustenance. To make the State our provider is to deny God. Herbert Schlossberg makes this point:

> The paternal state not only feeds its children, but nurtures, educates, comforts, and disciplines them, providing all they need for their security. This appears to be a mildly insulting way to treat adults, but it is really a great crime because it transforms the state from being a gift of God, given to protect us against violence, into an idol. It supplies us with all blessings, and we look to it for all our needs. Once we sink to that level, as [C.S.] Lewis says, there is no point in telling state officials to mind their own business. "Our whole lives *are* their business."[4]

---

4. Schlossberg, *Idols for Destruction*, 183–184.

Sad to say, there are millions of people, Christians included, who welcome and embrace a government that will take care of them. Of course, such a government attaches a high price tosuch benevolence.

As Christians, we have difficult decisions to make in every election year. I can't tell you how to vote but let me explain my decision-making process.

First, we do not believe that politics can save us, no matter how righteous a candidate might be, and no political candidate is even near perfect. The Bible says so, and so do the annals of history, the newspapers, internet news sources, and radio and television. This is true even in the church. Take a close look at the Bible at how God used the most imperfect of people to serve as judges, kings, and missionaries (Heb. 11; Gal. 2:11–14).

Second, weigh all the factors. It's easy to compare how the two major candidates stand on the issues. There are marked differences. In 2016, Hillary Clinton's positions were radically destructive on nearly every important issue; the same is true with Joe Biden in 2020. Here's just one example: Hillary's pro-abortion views and her support of Planned Parenthood were well known as are Joe Biden's and the Democratic Party who a similar position:

Hillary Clinton: "Under our laws... [t]he unborn person doesn't have constitutional rights."[5]

Donald Trump: If you go with what Hillary is saying [about partial-birth abortions], in the ninth month, you can take the baby and rip the baby out of the womb of the mother just prior to the birth of the baby.... Now, you can say that that's OK

---

5. See Gary DeMar, "Whoa. Hillary Clinton says Unborn Babies are People," Eagle Rising: https://bit.ly/39QLHHC

and Hillary can say that that's OK. But it's not OK with me, because based on what she's saying, and based on where she's going, and where she's been, you can take the baby and rip the baby out of the womb in the ninth month on the final day. And that's not acceptable.

Third, consider what each candidate brings to the office in terms of connections, political associations, special interest group support, corporations, and past actions that have political implications. It's easy to do since many of these candidates have a long record of opinions on social and political issues.

Fourth, how well will the more conservative and more biblically aligned party oppose the overtly unbiblical and unconstitutional policies advocated by the other party? Both parties and their supporters want a share of the goodies of fame, fortune, prestige, and power that come with their offices while ignoring deficits, debts, and decadence. Both parties will throw the people that support them a few crumbs and rub their bellies, and they'll go away wagging their tails happy with the scraps that fall from their master's table. There is a great deal of collusion between the two major parties.

Fifth, we're not electing a monarch, king, pastor, or god. We have a shared-power government with checks and balances. In terms of the Constitution, the President's authority is limited—at least it's supposed to be. The same is true of the Supreme Court. The way our political system is set up, it matters who is President because power is shared.

Sixth, what about third-party candidates? None of them has a chance of winning. We saw what happened when Ross Perot ran against George H.W. Bush and Bill Clinton in 1992. Perot's nearly 20 million votes most definitely affected the race since he got nearly half the votes of the two other candidates but did not receive a single electoral vote. Third party candidates do better at the local level.

Seventh, in the end, at this point in time, we're going to get either one of two presidential candidates from the two major parties. There is no third viable option at the national level.

In summary, does a less evil presidential candidate give us some breathing room to fix the many problems we face that are the result of government interference where it has no business being involved? A lot of damage has been done in the past few decades. This is especially true in the courts and the numerous bureaucracies and federal agencies that are the real power brokers in Washington.

> A major factor ... is whether one party or another is more likely to oppress Christians, to restrict their freedom (including freedom of worship, tax exempt status for churches, freedom to homeschool or send children to private Christian schools that aren't regulated by the government, etc.). As Peter Leithart once put it, which party is more likely to put me (or a godly pastor who preaches faithfully according to God's Word) into a concentration camp?[6]

Before long, there will be another election. The time is now to start teaching, training, and planning for the long-term. If you and I don't like today's choices, you and I need to get to work now to make sure it does not happen again.

---

6. Personal message to me from John Barach (September 18, 2020).

Nothing Matters
if This is True

Many are calling for a purely secular State. "Keep God out of government" is an often-repeated refrain. Is such a concept possible? There's always an ultimate authority behind every government and every law. Those who advocate for a godless State are only changing to a new god who becomes the ultimate authority in that society. R.J. Rushdoony put it this way:

> Law is in every culture *religious in origin.* Because law governs
> man and society, because it establishes and declares the meaning of justice and righteousness, law is inescapably religious, in
> that it establishes in practical fashion the ultimate concerns of
> a culture. Accordingly, a fundamental and necessary premise in
> any and every study of law must be, *first,* a recognition of this
> religious nature of law. *Second,* it must be recognized that in
> any culture *the source of law is the god of that society.*[1]

---

1. Rousas J. Rushdoony, *Institutes of Biblical Law* (Philadelphia, PA: Presby-

We're being told today that these things matter and those things matter, but without God, nothing actually and ultimately matters. Few people want to acknowledge that what we see happening today is a manifestation of the eternally present without any regard for an eternally just judicial system since there is no longer an ultimate Judge to judge. The framers of the Declaration of Independence recognized this truth when they appealed "to the Supreme Judge of the world for the rectitude of [their] intentions."

We've come a long way from 1776 when "life, liberty and the pursuit of happiness" were gifts from the "Creator" and had a transcendent reference point that resulted in moral permanence.

> CNN's Chris Cuomo ended a recent program telling viewers that America doesn't need God; that what we need is within us.
>
> "If you believe in one another and if you do the right thing for yourself and your community, things will get better in this country. You don't need help from above. It's within us," he said while pointing a finger to the sky.[2]

Who can say that anything is right or wrong if there is no universal objective definition of right and wrong? And where "within us" is the "right thing" found? The human body can be examined down to the molecular level and no one will find any "thing" that informs us what is right or wrong. When the true God is replaced with a manufactured temporal counterfeit, no lives ultimately matter except by the decree of the State. Atheist regimes during the twentieth century showed this to be true on a grand scale.

---

terian and Reformed, 1973), 4. Emphasis in original.

2. "CNN Anchor Chris Cuomo Says America Doesn't Need God," Movie Guide (July 1, 2020): https://bit.ly/3fvKoiF

I need to add that those who claim the name of the true God but do not follow His revealed laws are equally misguided and dangerous. There is a bloody trail of tyranny made by those who claim a divine right to the exclusion of keeping the law of God. The slave trade and wars are examples of godlessness in the name of God.

Why is the topic "Does God Exist?" important? Because it has both temporal and eternal significance. The late anti-theist Christopher Hitchens (1949–2011), the author of *God Is Not Great*, said that religious faith "will never die out, or at least not until we get over our fear of death, and of the dark, and of the unknown, and of each other."[3] Being afraid of the dark and other people do not have eternal consequences. The unknown can harbor uncertainties that should make us fearful, especially if the unknown means judgment based on what we do in this life. Hitchens had no empirical knowledge of what happens after death. Of course, he does now since he's dead.

What if atheists and anti-theists get their way and are able to eliminate a belief in God? What if belief in God was no more? Are their consequences to a fully consistent atheism—a molecule-to-man theory of evolutionary origins?

Hitchens was once asked this question: If atheists were so successful in making their case that God does not exist that only one believer was alive in the world, would he work to convert this last theist to atheism?"? Here was his answer as recorded in the debate film *Collision*,[4] which included interviews and debate

---

3. Christopher Hitchens, *God Is Not Great: How Religion Poisons Everything* (New York: Twelve Books/Hachette Book Group 2007), 12.

4. *Collision* (2009) can be viewed at https://bit.ly/3kEjPui. Douglas Wilson has also written *God Is: How Christianity Explains Everything* as a response to *God is Not Great*: https://bit.ly/2XEE56n

sequences between Hitchens and Christian apologist Douglas Wilson. The following appears at the end of the film:

> If I could convince everyone to be non-believers,...and there is only one [believer] left, one more, and then it would be done and there would be no more religion in the world and no more deism and theism, I wouldn't do it.

Fellow unbeliever and atheist high priest Richard Dawkins was astonished at Hitchens' answer:

> And Dawkins said, "What do you mean you wouldn't do it?" And I said I don't quite know why I wouldn't do it. And it is not just, because there would be nothing left to argue over and no one left to argue with, it is not just that, well, it would be then, somehow if I could drive it out of the world, I wouldn't and the incredulity with which he looked stays with me still, I've got to say.

I'll tell you why Hitchens wouldn't do it. Because living in a consistently atheistic world is impossible. Atheists talk about morality, goodness, and evil, but they can't account for them given their materialistic assumptions. This is not to say that today's atheists are not moral. They are and they aren't. They are because they assume a worldview that includes morality and the distinctions between good and evil. But how do you get morality from molecules and atoms? They aren't moral or immoral because atoms don't behave in a moral way, and, according to most atheists, we are nothing but "a bag of meat and bones"[5] animated by electricity. Morality is not a thing that can be put under the microscope.

---

5. "Kill Switch," *X-Files* (Season 5, Episode 11).

While reading about the latest Freedom From Religion lawsuit, I was watching *The Aviator* (2004), a film about Howard Hughes (1905–1976) that starred Leonardo DiCaprio and a bevy of other film stars. Hughes was an eccentric genius. He produced and directed films (*Scarface, Hell's Angels, The Outlaw*), owned Trans World Airlines (TWA) in the 1940s, was his own test pilot, and took on the Senate of the United States. He set multiple world air-speed records, built the Hughes H-1 Racer and H-4 "Hercules" (better known as the "Spruce Goose" because it was made out of wood and "spruce" and "goose" rhyme).

In addition to his business enterprises, Hughes was also known as something of a playboy. He kept company with numerous Hollywood stars: Katherine Hepburn, Ava Gardner, Ginger Rogers, Joan Fontaine, Linda Darnell, and Gene Tierney.

There's a scene in *The Aviator* where he and Katherine Hepburn (played by Cate Blanchett) discuss the ways of men and women in a Darwinian context. Hepburn was an atheist. Here's their conversion as they played a round of golf:

> **Hepburn:** "Heard you were wooing Ginger Rogers. What about that?"
>
> **Hughes:** "Ah, she's, uh, just a friend."
>
> **Hepburn:** "Ha! Men can't be friends with women, Howard. They must possess them or leave them be. It's a primitive urge from caveman days....It's all in Darwin. Hunt the flesh, kill the flesh, eat the flesh. That's the... male sex all over."

Hunt... kill... eat. "Are there any moral absolutes for beings that emerged by evolution from a biotic soup of chemicals if the entire process of evolution from molecules to man entailed hunting, killing, eating, and even raping the less fit?"

Later in the film, when Hepburn finds out that Hughes has been seeing other women, she turns on him for what she considers to be a moral affront. Hughes throws the earlier Darwin reference back at her. "You're the one that said that all men are predators. I mean, it's all in Darwin, remember?" Exactly! But Hepburn did not like the implications of her atheistic worldview when it was applied consistently to her.

There is temporal significance to a belief in an eternal "dirt nap" with no judgment to follow. If after death a mass murderer and a mass philanthropist receive the same end, why should there be a difference in their actions from this side of the grave? Late in life Hepburn told the *Ladies' Home Journal* in the October 1991 issue, "I'm an atheist, and that's it. I believe there's nothing we can know except that we should be kind to each other and do what we can for other people."

If there's nothing we can know, then how did she know about the kindness thing? Are we obligated to be kind to other people? Who ultimately makes the judgment if there is nothing greater than molecules in the vastness of the cosmos? Certainly, molecules aren't telling us to be kind. If they are, then what cosmic force told them, and why should we be morally obligated to obey a force? Hitchens argued that religious faith is the result of the evolutionary process.[6] Why can't the same thing be said for views of morality? What we conceive to be moral today can be immoral tomorrow. Maybe Adolf Hitler was ahead of the evolutionary curve, and we have not evolved enough to see what he saw.

Consider the following from John Lennox, Professor of Mathematics at Oxford University:

6. Hitchens, *God Is Not Great*, 12.

Science proceeds on the basis of the assumption that the universe is, at least to a certain extent, accessible to the human mind. No science can be done without the scientist believing this, so it is important to ask for grounds for this belief. Atheism gives us none, since it posits a mindless, unguided origin of the universe's life and consciousness.

Charles Darwin saw the problem. He wrote: "With me the horrid doubt always arises whether the convictions of man's mind, which has been developed from the mind of the lower animals, are of any value or at all trustworthy."[7]

Atheists are making their "this-is-the-only-life-you-have" worldview an advertising slogan. London buses have been outfitted with the following banner ads: "There's Probably No God. Now Stop Worrying and Enjoy Life."[8] The sponsors hoped the postings would get people to question the existence of God: "This campaign to put alternative slogans on London buses will make people think—and thinking is anathema to religion," the promoters argue. "[Richard] Dawkins said that as an atheist he 'wasn't wild' about the ad's assertion that there was 'probably' no God."[9] If there is no God, then who gets to say what constitutes enjoying life? Are there any restrictions on enjoying life? If there are, then who gets to set the restrictions and why?

The issue is not whether atheists are moral people. Some are, and some aren't. The more significant question is, How do athe-

---

7. "Why Atheism and Science Don't Mix," Evolution News (July 17, 2020): https://bit.ly/2RMygjG

8. Gwynne Dyer, "The Atheist Buses" (February 9, 2009): https://bit.ly/2YvbBfC

9. "Atheists Plan Anti-God Ad Campaign on Buses" (October 23, 2008): https://fxn.ws/3ldPFzl

ists account for morality given the fact they believe humans are a "mass" of evolved chunks of gooey matter that only look like they are designed.[10] For example, atheists collected donations for earthquake victims in Haiti. In a single day, an atheist charity received donations of $80,000 from as many as 3,400 donors. By day three they had raised $113,000. Atheist evangelist Richard Dawkins committed to matching donations up to $9,300.

Bravo! Other atheists could make a case that sending money to help people who can't help themselves is contrary to the survival of the fittest doctrine. Again, it's not that atheists can't do moral things; rather, it's that the things they do are not moral or immoral given the materialistic parameters and limitations of their worldview. Douglas Wilson explains it this way:

> One of the common features of these atheists is a very high level of moral indignation [against Christianity.] But given the premises of their worldview, they have no basis for their indignation. If there is no God, and everything is really just atoms banging around, why should it matter which way the atoms bang? Actually, all of these atheists surreptitiously borrow many of the standards of Christianity in order to assail Christian belief.[11]

An atheist is an "interloper on God's territory. Everything he uses to construct his system has been stolen from God's 'construction site.' The unbeliever is like the little girl who must climb on her father's lap to slap his face.... [T]he unbeliever must use the

---

10. Richard Dawkins, *The Greatest Show on Earth* (New York: Free Press, 2009), 371.

11. "Answering the 'new atheists': Lael Weinberger talks to *Doug Wilson*, author of *Letter from a Christian Citizen*": https://bit.ly/3lhqSdy

world as it has been created by God to try to throw God off His throne."[12] Atheists know they cannot be truthful about the full force of their worldview. Otherwise they would not be able to sell it to the world. Who, except an evolutionary scientist who has a career and reputation in the scientific community to protect, would identify with a worldview that is founded on a materialistic premise that claims that humans are a conglomeration of mixed atoms that have worms as one of their biological relatives, worse, that "the worm represents a very simple human"?[13]

According to prominent biochemist and Editor-in-Chief of *Science* magazine Dr. Bruce Alberts, our study of genes has made us "realize humans are more like worms than we ever imagined."[14] This is like saying the literary works of William Shakespeare and the novels of Amanda McKittrick Ros,[15] which

12. John A. Fielding III, "The Brute Facts: An Introduction of the Theology and Apologetics of Cornelius Van Til," *The Christian Statesman* 146:2 (March-April 2003), 30.

13. Glen Evans quoted in Sue Goetinck, "Methods used in worm study may help determine genetic blueprint of humans," Knight Ridder/Tribune News Service (December 11, 1998). This quotation can also be found in John G. West, *Darwin Day in America: How Our Politics and Culture have Been Dehumanized in the Name of Science* (Wilmington, DE: Intercollegiate Studies Institute, 2007), 4. West's bibliographic reference has the Evans' citation appearing in Nicholas Wade, "Animal's Genetic Program Decoded, in a Science First," *New York Times* (December 11, 1998): https://nyti.ms/2FRMxsK (I was not able to find it in this article.)

14. Quoted in Wade, "Animal's Genetic Program Decoded, in a Science First." The Bible identifies humans as worms (Ps. 22:6; cf. Job 24:6; Isa. 41:14); but it is making a theological point, not a biological one.

15. Just like there is a "Golden Turkey Award" for films (Ed Wood's *Plan 9 from Outer Space* (1959) took top honors), there seems to be one for writers. Nick Page is the author of *In Search of the World's Worst Writers*. Ros is at the top of the list. "She refers to eyes as 'globes of glare,' legs as 'bony supports,' pants as a 'southern necessary,' sweat as 'globules of liquid lava' and alcohol as the 'powerful monster of mangled might.' The Oxford literary group "The Inklings," which included C. S. Lewis and J.R.R. Tolkien, held competitions to see who could read

Mark Twain described as "hogwash literature," are comparable because they use the same 26 letters of the English alphabet or that *Plan 9 from Outer Space* and *District 9* are artistically similar because they both have the number "9" in the title. The fact that other life forms have DNA and that some or even much of it is found in humans in no way means that worms, bananas, or chimpanzees are in any way related to humans. All automobiles share common functioning parts, but this does not mean they are related by evolutionary extension.

The rigorously consistent evolutionist is left with treating humans as highly functioning sound machines.

> The story is told of a visit of the behaviourist psychologist Professor Burrhus Skinner to lecture at Keele University [in England]. After Skinner had given his formal lecture, in which he emphasized an objective, mechanistic description as a total explanation of man's behaviour, he was invited to have an informal chat with the professor who had chaired the meeting. Skinner was asked whether in fact he was at all interested in who he, the chairman, and others were. Implacable, Skinner replied: "I am interested in the noises that come from your mouth."[16]

Skinner was trying to be as consistent as his deterministic worldview would allow him to be. There are no words with real meaning that emanate from one of our frontal orifices; they are only noises. Similarly, the same can be said for moral attributes. They can only be observed and noted as things that these flesh

---

her work aloud longest while keeping a straight face." (Miles Corwin, "Words to Remember," *Smithsonian* [June 2009]).

16. Denis Alexander, *Beyond Science* (Philadelphia: A.J. Holman Co., 1972), 45.

and blood sound machines emit. So even if objective moral standards were proven to exist in a world explained in terms of atheistic assumptions, there is no inherent obligation to observe any of them.

Abortion, Biblical Law, and the Civil Magistrate

The topic of abortion has become an absolute dividing line in today's political wars. The Democratic Party believes a woman should have the legal right to kill her unborn baby anytime up to conception on the grounds of "mental health." A new Virginia law includes the following that would permit an unborn baby to be aborted if "the continuation of the pregnancy is likely to result in the death of the woman or **impair the mental** or physical health of the woman." All a woman would have to do is declare that her mental health would be impaired if she delivers her baby alive. That's a slippery slope loophole if there ever was one.

Virginia Governor Ralph Northam, a former pediatric neurologist, when asked what would happen if a disabled baby survived the abortion attempt, said the following:

> The infant would be delivered. The infant would be kept comfortable. The infant would be resuscitated if that's what the

mother and the family desired. And then a discussion would ensue between the physicians and the mother.[1]

Ostensibly conservative Christian writers and theologians supported the Democratic presidential ticket in the 2020 election. Consider the following from someone who worked for Ohio Right to Life:

> A pro-life spokeswoman quit her job rather than endorse Donald Trump for another term in the White House. Trump has called himself the most pro-life president in history. But Stephanie Ranade Krider, executive director for Ohio Right to Life, decided she couldn't support him and couldn't keep working for the prominent pro-life group as it prepared to help him win re-election.[2]

Krider claims to hold an anti-abortion position even though the Trump administration came out clearly against abortion, something the Democratic Party has not done.

- Continue nominating constitutionalist Supreme Court and lower court judges
- Protect unborn life through every means available
- Defend the freedoms of religious believers and organizations

Democratic nominee Joe Biden has promised to defend abortion rights as "women's healthcare," supports the 1973 pro-abortion *Roe v. Wade* decision, and continues to call for the funding of

1. Quoted in Devan Cole, "Virginia governor faces backlash over comments supporting late-term abortion bill" (January 31, 2019): https://cnn.it/34Fht9Y

2. Daniel Silliman, "On the Front Lines, Some Pro-Life Activists Think Twice About Supporting Trump," *Christianity Today* (September 1, 2020): https://bit.ly/2EVTJDG

pro-abortion Planned Parenthood by forcing American taxpayers to fund abortions. Consider the following interview with the editorial board at *The New York Times* in January 2020 when he was asked what he would look for in a Supreme Court nominee:

> [T]hey have to . . . acknowledge the unenumerated rights and a right to privacy in the Constitution, and the "penumbra" [laws that don't actually appear in the Constitution] and the Ninth Amendment, then in fact that means I know they will, in fact, support *Roe v. Wade*. They'll support a woman's right to choose. . . . That is critical. I've written about it extensively. I've written law review articles about it. I've presided over more judges and more Supreme Court nominees than anybody else has. Look at the people I supported. *When I defeated [Robert] Bork [as a Supreme Court Justice in 1987], I was able to provide a woman's right for a generation because had he won, it would have been over.*[3]

Contrary to Stephanie Ranade Krider's attack on the Trump administration, Carol Tobias, president of National Right to Life, "said without hesitation that 'the administration has done a fantastic job.' In addition to the appointments of lower court judges, Trump has 'sent a clear message, not just to the country but to the entire world, that this administration is going to fight for the rights of the unborn,' Tobias said. 'This is more than symbolism from the administration. They're working hard and they're doing what they can. . . . But I think the symbolism is important too, and it's helping.'"[4]

---

3. Quoted in Laura Echevarria, "Joe Biden: My Supreme Court Judges Will Support a "Right" to Kill Babies in Abortions" (Sept. 11, 2020). Emphasis added: https://bit.ly/35vzaJC

4. Silliman, "On the Front Lines."

CAN A "DEVOUT CHRISTIAN" SUPPORT ABORTION ON DEMAND?

Former seminary and college professor Tremper Longman III claimed that pro-abortion advocate Joe Biden "is a devout Christian by all accounts." All accounts? Supporting abortion on demand is not in any way a Christian view. The Democratic Party platform position supports abortion on demand. A "devout Christian" could not run on or vote for such a platform.

Many Christians engaged politically when the 1973 *Roe v. Wade* pro-abortion case was decided. At first, there was a visceral reaction to the decision since abortion has been looked upon as a criminal offense. Of course, this did not stop women from getting abortions illegally. Prior to *Roe v. Wade* abortion was illegal in thirty states and legal under certain circumstances in thirty states.

While a visceral reaction to abortion was helpful, it did not ask the more fundamental question about what the Bible says on the subject. Tremper Longman III writes that "[t]he Bible does not speak directly to the issue of abortion or . . . clearly about the status of a fetus in the womb."[5] I'll take up his reasoning below.

ABORTION, THE BIBLE, AND THE "CHRISTIAN RIGHT"

Those attempting to support abortion have encountered biblical arguments and attempt to refute them with twisted exegesis and unreliable history. For example, Jacob Shelton, writing for the website Weird History, claims that the translation of Exodus

---

5. Tremper Longman III, *The Bible and the Ballot: Using Scripture in Political Decisions* (Grand Rapids, MI: Eerdmans, 2020), 136.

21:22–25 was altered to support the GOP and the Christian Right because of their anti-abortion stance:

> In the 1975 version of the *New American Standard Bible,* the verse read: "And if men struggle with each other and strike a woman with child so that **she has a miscarriage**, yet there is not further injury, he shall surely be fined as the woman's husband may demand of him; and he shall pay as the judges decide."
>
> In 1995, the verse was changed to read: "If men struggle with each other and strike a woman with child so that **she gives birth prematurely,** yet there is no injury...."

The words were changed in the 1995 version in order to make it so the fetus doesn't die in the verse, thus supporting the Christian Right's pro-life message that killing a fetus is the same as killing a human, and the Bible says so.

Shelton may be "a know it all when it comes to horror movies, serial killers, government conspiracies, comic books, and movies about comic books," as he describes himself, but he does not know much about the Bible and Bible translations.

The goal of translating the Bible into another language is to make it as accurate, readable, and accessible as possible for people who can't read the original languages. Every translation has gone through revisions, even the KJV. In fact, every new translation that is published is an attempt to make the original languages of Hebrew, Aramaic, and Greek a better translation of the original. Some translations try to do this by smoothing out the original language to get the essence of the meaning while others try to be as literal as possible without being wooden. That's why you will see in some translations (e.g., KJV and NASB) words printed in *italic* to indicate that they are not in the original language. They are added to make a passage more understandable.

Let's put Mr. Shelton's claim that the NASB editors changed its translation of Exodus 21:22 for political reasons to the test.

BIBLICAL CASE LAW: LEX TALIONIS

First, Exodus 21:22–25 deals with a judicial case where two men struggle (fight) with each other. We are not told why they are fighting. A pregnant woman is standing near enough to them that she is affected by the altercation. She goes into premature labor. This case law covers all the "cases," everything from no harm to the mother and her prematurely born children (plural) to harm resulting in death to the mother and one or more of her unborn children.

Second, the woman is not deciding to have an abortion. At one level, it's an accident that she goes into labor. There is no premeditation on her part. At another level, however, the men should not have been fighting, so there is some liability on their part. The woman could be the wife of one of the men who is trying to break up the fight.

Even if there is a distinction in terms of harm to the mother and the unborn child in what is ostensibly an accidental act, this is a far cry from permitting women to intentionally kill their unborn children up until the end-point of a normal pregnancy.

Notice that this Mosaic regulation had to do with injury inflicted indirectly and **accidentally**: "The phrasing of the case suggests that we are dealing with an instance of unintentional battery involving culpability" (Michael Fishbane, *Biblical Interpretation in Ancient Israel* (New York: Oxford University Press, 1985), 92). Abortion, on the other hand, is a **deliberate, purposeful, intentional** termination of a child's life. If God dealt severely with the **accidental** death of a pre-born infant, how do you suppose He feels about the **deliberate** murder of the unborn by an abortion doctor in collusion with the mother? The Bible states explicitly how He feels: "[D]o not kill the innocent and righteous. For I will not justify the wicked" (Exodus 23:7). As a matter of fact, one of the things that God **hates** is "hands that shed innocent blood" (Proverbs 6:17; cf. 2 Kings 8:12; 15:16; Hosea 13:16; Amos 1:13). Abortion is a serious matter with God. We absolutely must base our views on **God's** will—not the will of men. The very heart and soul of this great nation is being ripped out by unethical actions like abortion. We must return to the Bible as our standard of behavior—before it is everlastingly too late.[6]

Third, the text is clear, she is pregnant with at least one child: "And if men struggle with each other and strike a woman with child...." (Ex. 21:22). The Brown-Driver-Briggs *Hebrew-English Lexicon* defines *hareh* as a pregnant woman with child. It's clear that she is not carrying around a mass of undefined tissue that **becomes** a human being when "it" exits the sanctuary of the womb.

Fourth, the Bible attributes self-consciousness to unborn babies, something that modern medicine has studied and acknowledged. Jacob and Esau "struggled together within" their

---

6. Dave Mill, "Abortion and Exodus 21," Apologetics Press: https://bit.ly/33ix90y

mother's womb (Gen. 25:22). The New Testament offers a similar glimpse into prenatal consciousness: "And it came about that when Elizabeth heard Mary's greeting, the baby leaped in her womb" (Luke 1:41). "Struggling" and "leaping" are the result of consciousness. Jacob and Esau fighting inside the womb is indicative of their continued fighting outside the womb. John leaps in reaction to Mary's pregnancy.

Fifth, some commentators claim that in Exodus 21:22 the death of a "fetus," either accidentally or on purpose, is nothing more than a property crime rather than the killing of a human being. The Bible teaches otherwise. The original Hebrew reads: "And if men struggle with each other and strike a pregnant woman so that her **children** [*yeled*] come out...." Notice that the text uses the word "children," not "products of conception." The Hebrew word for "children" in this verse is used in other contexts to designate a child already born. For example, in Exodus 2:6 we read: "When Pharaoh's daughter opened [the basket], she saw the child [*yeled*], and behold, the boy was crying. And she had pity on him and said, 'This is one of the Hebrews' children [*yeled*].'" Since in the Exodus case these are "*children that come out*," they are persons, not body parts like an appendix or a kidney.

Sixth, if there is no injury to these individuals—the mother and her prematurely delivered child or children—then there is no penalty. If there is injury, then the judges must decide on an appropriate penalty based on the extent of the injury either to the mother and/or her child because both are persons in terms of biblical law.

Seventh, some translations have "so that she has a miscarriage." As Shelton points out, the 1977 edition of the New American Standard Bible on the passage in question used "miscarriage." The 1995 translation is better ("she gives birth prematurely"), but it still does not capture the literal rendering of the Hebrew. In a marginal note, the NASB translators recognize that the literal meaning of the text is "her children come out."

It's frustrating to read translations that include marginal notes telling us what it *really* says *literally*. Translate it literally, and then use the margin to offer an explanation if needed. Other translations have a more word-for-word translation. Here's one example from the Holman Christian Standard Bible:

> When men get in a fight and hit a pregnant woman **so that her children are born** [prematurely] but there is no injury, the one who hit her must be fined as the woman's husband demands from him, and he must pay according to judicial assessment.

Notice that it's "so that her **children** are born." Here's another from *Young's Literal Translation* (1898):

> "And when men strive, and have smitten a pregnant woman, and **her children have come out**, and there is no mischief, he is certainly fined, as the husband of the woman doth lay upon him, and he hath given through the judges."

Note the date (1898), long before there was a Christian Right, long before abortion became a national moral tragedy when the Supreme Court legalized abortion in 1973.

Eighth, there are two Hebrew words that fit the circumstances of miscarriage or premature birth: "There shall be no one miscarrying [*shakal*] or barren in your land" (Ex. 23:26; also, Hosea 9:14). The Hebrew word for "miscarriage" was available to Moses since it appears just two chapters later. Another example is found in Job: "Or like a miscarriage [*nefel*] which is discarded, I would not be" (Job 3:16). Meredith G. Kline offers a helpful summary of the passage:

> This law found in Exodus 21:22–25 turns out to be perhaps the most decisive positive evidence in scripture that the fetus is to be regarded as a living person.... No matter whether one interprets the first or second penalty to have reference to a miscarriage, there is no difference in the treatments according to the fetus and the woman. Either way the fetus is regarded as a living person, so that to be criminally responsible for the destruction of the fetus is to forfeit one's life.... The fetus, at any stage of development, is, in the eyes of this law, a living being, for life (*nephesh*) is attributed to it.... Consistently in the relevant data of Scripture a continuum of identity is evident between the fetus and the person subsequently born and Exodus 21:22–25 makes it clear that this prenatal human being is to be regarded as a separate and distinct human life.[7]

Umberto Cassuto, also known as Moshe David Cassuto (1883–1951), was a Jewish rabbi and biblical scholar born in Florence, Italy. In his commentary on Exodus, he presents an accurate translation of the passage based on the nuances of the Hebrew:

> When men strive together and they hurt unintentionally a woman with child, and her children come forth but no mischief happens—that is, the woman and the children do not die—the one who hurts her shall surely be punished by a fine.

---

7. Meredith G. Kline, "*Lex Talionis* and the Human Fetus," *The Simon Greenleaf Law Review*, 5 (1985–1986), 75, 83, 88–89. This article originally appeared in *Journal of the Evangelical Theological Society* (September 1977). Also see H. Wayne House, "Miscarriage or Premature Birth: Additional Thoughts on Exodus 21:22-25," *Westminster Theological Journal*, 41:1 (Fall 1978), 108–123.

But if any mischief happens, that is, if the woman dies or the children, then you shall give life for life.[8]

Note the date: 1967. Before *Roe v. Wade* and before the rise of the so-called Christian Right. Cassuto was a Jew and not a Christian.

Ninth, the King James Version takes a different translation approach, but it is consistent with the text that "children" are "coming out." The KJV reads, "If men strive, and hurt a woman with child, so that **her fruit** depart *from her*, and yet no mischief follow: he shall be surely punished, according as the woman's husband will lay upon him; and he shall pay as the judges *determine*" (Ex. 21:22). The use of the word "fruit" is a descriptive euphemism for a child in the Old Testament (Gen. 30:2) and the New Testament (Luke 1:42). Elizabeth responded to Mary in the following way when she learned of Mary's pregnancy:

And she spake out with a loud voice, and said, Blessed art thou among women, and blessed is the **fruit of thy womb**.

Mr. Shelton needs to do a bit more investigative digging before he publishes fake history and fake exegesis as real exegesis.

"DO HARM" OR "FULLY FORMED"?

One additional translation point needs to be discussed. Tremper Longman takes the position based on translation ambiguity that "[t]he safest conclusion is that [Exodus 21:22–25] should not be used as a prooftext in support of either a pro-choice or

---

8. Umberto Cassuto, *Commentary on the Book of Exodus* (Jerusalem: Magnes Press, The Hebrew University, 1967), 275.

pro-life position."[9] He argues that the passage does not regard the unborn child (fetus) as fully a person throughout his or her development in the womb. It's only when the unborn baby is fully formed that personhood can be attributed to the fetus. At what point does a fetus become "fully formed" so "it" becomes a person? Who gets to make that decision and based on what criteria? Again, for the Democratic Party the "fully formed" distinction is irrelevant since a woman can decide to kill her unborn baby anytime during her pregnancy.

Longman diverges from the Hebrew text and argues that since the Septuagint was used in Jesus' day, and "was the main translation used not only by Jewish readers but also by the disciples and the early followers of Jesus who did not read Hebrew,"[10] therefore its translation is authoritative for us over against the Hebrew.

The New Testament writers don't use the Septuagint exclusively. Jesus and the New Testament writers quote from the Hebrew text and the Septuagint. Jesus quotes a part of Exodus 21:24 in Matthew 5:38, but the Hebrew text and Septuagint translation agree. The writers are selective in what they quote. It does not mean that the Septuagint as a whole is authoritative. In addition, there are numerous deviations from the Hebrew text that obscure Christian doctrines that are essential to the faith. "The upshot of all this is that the Septuagint should not be preferred to the Masoretic at every turn. At very least the Septuagint should be used along with the Masoretic."[11]

---

9. Longman, *The Bible and the Ballot*, 141.
10. Longman, *The Bible and the Ballot*, 142.
11. Fr. Lawrence Farley, "Reflections on the Septuagint," No Other Foundation (March 29, 2018): https://bit.ly/35wkjOQ

There's also the possibility that a "NT writer may have been making his own translation of a Hebrew text (or an Aramaic translation—a *targum*—for that matter), quoting or paraphrasing from memory, or making a deliberate change for his own theological reasons." In addition:

> A careful analysis of the NT quotations of the OT reveals that practically every quotation has at least minor variants from the Septuagints[12] (or major ones) and is never verbatim. That is significant. Either the NT writers were using different Greek manuscripts to the extant versions of the Septuagints or something else was happening. If the Greek Jewish Scriptures were regarded so highly by the NT writers why do they appear to be so careless in quoting it (if they were indeed quoting it) so as to have so many variants? There isn't a single quote in the entire New Testament which quotes verbatim from any Septuagint manuscripts that we have....
>
> [From a number of examples] I think we could conclude that the NT writers were either using a different Greek text to our Septuagints, they were making their own translation from the Hebrew, or they were using a Septuagint but changing it or improving it as they went....[13]

The following translation from some Septuagint version of Exodus 21:22–25 is from Longman's book *The Bible and the Ballot*:

> If two men fight and they strike a woman who is pregnant, and her child comes out **while not yet fully formed**, he will be forced to pay a fine; whatever the woman's husband imposes, he

---

12. There is no single authoritative Septuagint.

13. Stephen Cook, "Does the New Testament always quote from the Septuagint?" (April 16, 2013): https://bit.ly/2FvMhQ5

will pay with a valuation. But **if it is fully formed**, he will give life for life, eye for eye, tooth for tooth, hand for hand, foot for foot, burning for burning, wound for would, stripe for stripe.

Instead of translating the Hebrew word *'ason* as "harm," the Septuagint translates it as "not yet fully formed." This is not a translation but an interpretation. The Samaritan Pentateuch, like the Septuagint, differs from the Hebrew Masoretic Text in numerous places but agrees with the Hebrew on Exodus 21:22–25:

If men strive, and hurt a woman with child, so that her fruit depart from her, and yet **no mischief** follow: he shall be surely punished, according as the woman's husband will lay upon him; and he shall pay as the judges determine. And if any **mischief** follow, then thou shalt give life for life, eye for eye, tooth for tooth, hand for hand, foot for foot, smiting for smiting, wound for wound, stripe for stripe.

The translation issue between the Hebrew Text and Septuagint comes down to the following:

How did the Septuagint come to translate the Hebrew word *'ason* ('harm') by the Greek word *exeikonismenon* ('fully formed')? Many scholars have pointed to the influence of Greek philosophical ideas. For Aristotle, an unformed embryo was not yet a human being. If the foetus is 'fully formed' then miscarriage would harm a human being. However, if it is unformed then it is not yet human and so there is no serious harm. This seems to be the underlying idea.

The claim is made by Thomas F. McDaniel that "[o]nce upon a time there were two distinctly different Hebrew words which were spelled consonantly as וֹסאָ. There was the well-rec-ognized וֹסָאָ, cited in all the standard Hebrew lexicons,...[14] There was also another וֹסאָ in the early Israelite and Alexan-drian dialects of Hebrew which became lost in the later Judean and Samaritan Hebrew dialects."[15] As far as I have been able to determine, McDaniel does not offer any evidence for his claim. "Once upon a time" is not evidence.

Following the Septuagint translation, "fully formed" only applies to the fetus. This means that nothing is being said about the mother in Exodus 21:22–25. What if she is injured? Ac-cording to the Septuagint translation, she is not considered in the judicial judgment since "fully formed" does not apply to her. The use of the Hebrew *'ason* ("harm") applies to the mother and unborn child (see above). The Septuagint has gone beyond translation to interpretation.

DEMOCRATS SUPPORT ABORTING "FULLY FORMED" BABIES

The major problem with Longman's view on the abortion issue in his support for Biden and the Democratic Party is that the Democrats believe that even a "fully formed" fetus can be killed. This is hardly the Christian position even by Septuagint trans-lation standards. Since the Democratic Party supports abortion throughout a woman's pregnancy it would mean that the abor-

---

14. See *sub voce*: (a) Francis Brown, S. R. Driver, and C. A. Briggs, *A Hebrew and English Lexicon of the Old Testament with an Appendix Containing the Biblical Aramaic*; (b) David J. A. Clines, *The Dictionary of Classical Hebrew*; and (c) Ludwig Koehler and W. Baumgartner, *The Hebrew and Aramaic Lexicon of the Old Testament*.

15. Thomas F. McDaniel, "The Septuagint Has the Correct Translation of Exodus 21:22–23" (2012): https://bit.ly/3mf9iaB

tion of Jacob and Esau, John the Baptist, and Jesus would have been lawful any time up to birth. Longman certainly does not believe the Bible or common sense would support such a position, but that's the political party he is supporting.

In the final analysis, the Democratic Party supports the right of the mother to kill the baby in the sancturary of the mother's womb even when fully formed. In addition, the Democratic Party is calling for the end of the Hyde Amendment that prohibited tax dollars being used to pay for abortions. Here's how Rep. Barbara Lee, a Democrat from Oakland, CA, defends taxpayer funding of abortion:

> It's an issue of racial justice and it's an issue of discrimination against low-income women, women of color, women who don't have access to what middle- and upper-income women have in terms of the choice to have an abortion.[16]

In the United States, the abortion rate for black women is almost five times that of white women. "The Black Panthers in the early 1970s claimed that legalized abortion would 'destroy our people.' Jesse Jackson, in a 1970s interview with *Jet* magazine, characterized abortion as 'black genocide.'"[17]

Stephanie Ranade Krider, who I mentioned earlier in this Appendix, says she cannot support President Trump. Here are some of her reasons: "Always, there has been this undercurrent where he just does not respect women and he does not like black and brown people." There is no factual evidence that this

---

16. Quoted in Jennifer Haberkorn, "House Democrats will try to repeal long-standing ban on federal money for abortions," *Los Angeles Times* (August 28, 2020): https://lat.ms/3hlKMBf

17. "Pro-birth isn't synonymous with pro-life," *The Telegraph* (March 7, 2014): https://bit.ly/3mfdMxX

is true. In the 2020 election, President Trump had the highest support from black voters than any Republican presidential candidate has ever had. If she is interested in supporting "black and brown people," how could she support a political party that supports paying for abortions of unborn black and brown babies with taxper money?

Psalm 139:13–16

For You formed my inward parts;
　You wove me in my mother's womb.
I will give thanks to You, for I am fearfully and wonderfully made;
　Wonderful are Your works,
And my soul knows it very well.
　My frame was not hidden from You,
When I was made in secret,
　And skillfully wrought in the depths of the earth;
Your eyes have seen my unformed substance;
　And in Your book were all written
The days that were ordained for me,
　When as yet there was not one of them.